JOURNEY WITH THE WORLD'S BEST TRAVEL WRITERS

Fill in this card and we'll let you know about the best travel stories we've found.

Which book did this card come from? _____

Name _____

Company (optional) _____

Mailing Address _____

City/State _____

Zip/Country _____

Telephone _____

Email address _____

We have other Travelers' Tales in the works. What other countries, regions, or topics interest you?

_____

Did you buy this book to:
- ☐ Prepare for a trip   ☐ Class/Seminar   ☐ Armchair Travel
- ☐ Interest in a specific region or topic   ☐ Gift

Where did you purchase your copy?
- ☐ Bookstore   ☐ Direct from O'Reilly   ☐ Received as gift   ☐ Online   ☐ Other

☐ Please send me the Travelers' Tales Catalog
☐ I do not want my name given to outside mailing lists

Give us three names and addresses of people you think would like Travelers' Tales and we will enter your name in our monthly drawing to receive one free Travelers' Tales book of your choice!

Name _____
Address _____
City/State/Zip _____

Name _____
Address _____
City/State/Zip _____

Name _____
Address _____
City/State/Zip _____

TRAVELERS' TALES

"Like gourmet chefs sampling the produce in an overstocked French market, the editors of Travelers' Tales pick, sift, and prod their way through the weighty shelves of contemporary travel writing, rejecting the second rate and creaming off the very best. They have impeccable taste—a very welcome addition to the genre."

—*William Dalrymple, author of City of Djinns and In Xanadu*

TRAVELERS' TALES

A DOG'S WORLD

TRAVELERS' TALES

A DOG'S
WORLD

Collected and Edited by

CHRISTINE HUNSICKER

Series Editors
JAMES O'REILLY AND LARRY HABEGGER

TRAVELERS' TALES, INC.
SAN FRANCISCO, CALIFORNIA

Distributed by
O'REILLY AND ASSOCIATES, INC.
101 MORRIS STREET
SEBASTOPOL, CALIFORNIA 95472

Plus on apprend à connaître l'homme,
plus on apprend à estimer le chien.

The more one gets to know them,
the more one values dogs.

—A. TOUSSENEL

Table of Contents

Part Two
A DOG'S LIFE AROUND THE WORLD

Preface

Most of us are outsiders when we travel. Whether we are traveling through a foreign country or just to a neighboring state, we are apart from the places we visit. Until we make a connection. For some travelers, a bond is established by a mutual friend or relative; for others a shared interest, or experience, provides the nexus. For many of us the magic link to a sense of belonging, even in the most unlikely of places, is made by a dog. Whether we travel with our own pets or encounter dogs in another land and culture, our experience is enriched through them and in meeting other people who revel in the company of dogs.

We travel with our canine counterparts for a variety of reasons. Many of us want to avoid The Look and subsequent guilt when leaving our beloved pets behind at home. Some of us appreciate a dog's great skill as a conversational ice-breaker, providing common ground and a reason—an excuse—to socially interact with complete strangers. Some of us take along our buddies just for the companionship they offer up so effortlessly and unfailingly.

In a former work life, I spent six years driving throughout the Western U.S. as a sales representative for a book publisher. Whenever possible, and sometimes even when it wasn't, I would bring along Arthur, my beloved shepherd lab. He stood guard over me during our layovers in low-budget motels located in the middle of nowhere and at those remote, secluded Interstate rest stops. He made me laugh; he made me exercise. He even gave me credibility to booksellers who had never met me before. When I retired from life on the road, Arthur became my "au paw," helping me keep track of my children on family camping trips or helping me keep my sanity and sense of humor as we chauffeured a vanful of chil-

dren about town. A car trip without Arthur was unthinkable to either of us.

In putting together this collection I wanted the stories to reflect
the many roles dogs take on as they travel the road of life with us.
You will meet a traveling companion for a cross-country horseback
rider, a sled leader in the Alaskan Iditarod, and a highly trained
guide for a visually impaired woman expanding her horizons.

In her introduction, Maria Goodavage, who has written a number of the Dog Lover's travel guides, describes how she and her dog
Joe started traveling together and the benefits gained by both of
them as a result. Many stories in this book relate travel experiences
that were greatly changed as a result of having a dog or two along
as company. Sometimes life-saving, sometimes life-changing, but
always a different experience from what the writers would have
had on their own.

About the time I stopped long-distance traveling with Arthur,
my mother returned from a trip to China with a sad but altogether
true tale about a puppy market she had seen there. It seemed impossible the same animal that had become my therapist and best
friend could be someone's dinner in another part of the world.
Didn't these people know what they were missing?

I became curious about the fate of dogs all over the world.
France is famous for the lavish treatment of its dogs, and tales of
dogs dining at—not even under—the table in Maxim's are leg-
endary. But what about dogs in other lands?

So I also looked for essays that explored a dog's life in other parts
of the world. As incredible as it seems to any dog lover, there are
countries in the world—usually poor nations with limited food resources—where dogs are viewed as livestock, food for starving citizens. There are, too, the cultural differences to bear in mind. Many
societies revile dogs, considering them outcasts and unclean, to be
avoided at all times. And yet, even in those dog-hostile environ-
ments, the human-canine bond of love and trust can overcome tradition. Dog lovers might be more universal than one would think
and there are tributes to dogs where least expected. In her story
"Going to the Dogs" one writer shares with us her journey to

Nepal where each year one day of a five-day celebration honoring animals is set aside to celebrate dogs. And in Japan, where many dogs are doted upon like children, one homesick writer succumbs to a local custom and "rents" a dog in "The Things We Do for Love." Even in China things finally seem to be looking up again for the animal once cherished by dynastic emperors.

It is important to keep in mind that the travel essays in this book are written by individuals and reflect only their particular experiences. The authors come from many walks of life. They are writers, dog breeders, teachers, retirees, trek leaders, and computer programmers. They are, for the most part, dog lovers of the highest order who want to see this magnificent species elevated to their rightful spot in the world—by our side, always.

Travelers' Tales: A Dog's World is organized simply. In Part One, "Traveling Tails," are stories about traveling with dogs, some humorous, some heartening, each one describing how a trip was changed, usually for the better, by the companionship of a dog. Part Two, "A Dog's Life Around the World," provides a look at a dog's life and role in society around the world. In Part Three, "Some Things to Do," the stories reflect places and activities that dog lovers have found to be fun or meaningful. Part Four, "In the Shadows," reflects some of the unfortunate things that can happen on the road with our dogs or in another culture that doesn't regard dogs in the same way we do. Part Five, "The Last Word," is just that, a grace note reflecting the many roles that dogs hold in our lives and in our world.

In the back of the book is a section entitled "The Next Step: Tips and Guidelines for Traveling with Your Dog." In addition to travel advice we've included some dog-related resources in "The Internet Unleashed." The World Wide Web is a wonderful place to connect with other dog enthusiasts. If you have always wanted to hook up to the Web but have been too intimidated to try, take heart. It's not as difficult as you might think. If you are already on-line, I hope this section will provide you with some new cyber tools to navigate new territory in the world of dogs.

We've also included a section, "Recommended Reading," to

provide you with a listing of books and other travel resources that will help you plan your next trip and make it easier for you to take along your own canine companion.

And it is my hope that after reading this book, you will take your dog along for the ride. Happy trails to you all.

—CHRISTINE HUNSICKER

A Dog's World: An Introduction

BY MARIA GOODAVAGE

It was Joe's second cousin who was responsible for Joe's lack of travel the first year of his life. Every time I closed the door on Joe's pleading face, I thought of Cousin Whiz, an Airedale with a strange streak a mile long, and reasoned that I was doing the right thing. After all, if Cousin Whiz could somehow escape from a locked vehicle and taunt traffic on Interstate 5 with the temerity of a *toreador*—not once, but twice—Joe could too.

Cousin Whiz made no bones about the fact that he was a tough-traveling terrier. As soon as his folks, Ed and Zoe Rogers, parked their 40-foot-long recreational vehicle in front of our San Francisco home and opened the door, Cousin Whiz would bolt straight through our gate and stand stock still while Joe, eight years his junior, sniffed him from tail to nose.

"Check out my snout, Cuz," anyone who watched would swear Whiz was saying. "This mouth has tasted water from toilets from Maine to California. And note the scent on my right front foot. Hah! That's the closest you'll ever come to setting paw in a canoe on the Suwannee River." With each area Joe sniffed, Cousin Whiz would stand straighter and prouder and puff up ever so slightly.

Whiz's folks, energetic retirees armed with hundreds of pooper scoopers, were as proud of Cousin Whiz's achievements as Whiz was. They referred to themselves as his chauffeurs, and laughed like parents of a naughty child prodigy when discussing his escapades on—and in—the road. The conversations about their cross-country treks were always punctuated by tales of Cousin Whiz (who would have been named after John Steinbeck's traveling poodle Charley, but Zoe's brother was named Charlie and he would have gotten upset at Whiz taking his name, especially since Brother

Charlie was also slightly strange and had madly curly hair, a brown beard, and deep-set brown eyes):

"How Whiz escaped and got onto the highway from the back of the RV we'll never know. We think he opened a window. My god, what a dog."

"That sunrise off Mount Katahdin with Whiz on our laps was the most beautiful experience we've ever had—short of our kids being born of course."

"Remember when Whiz charmed that gallery owner in Santa Fe and he gave us that beautiful clown painting? What a dog."

Regardless of the tale, Zoe always had a way of making the conversation lead to the same point: "Honey, you haven't traveled 'til you've traveled with a dog. It's hard to explain," she'd say, with a look of a child reveling in a mystery. "Whiz has opened our eyes like you couldn't even imagine."

Whiz had indeed opened their eyes, and the eyes of some innocent bystanders as well. It's nothing short of an eye-opener when a dog drags the beach blanket from under an impassioned couple in San Diego, or when he steals the walking stick of one of the most prominent citizens in Birmingham.

I wasn't sure that I was up for traveling with Joe. After all, he shared more than a few genes with Cousin Whiz. But it was getting harder to leave Joe home with a pet sitter when I embarked on road trips, and I'm sure Whiz's visits had something to do with this; Joe was quickly becoming an expert in the art of giving guilt; his tale drooped and his eyes grew deeper and wetter as I approached the door.

So instead of going alone to a Northern California venue for a newspaper assignment one weekend, I succumbed to the guilt and brought Joe along. Within minutes of crossing the Golden Gate Bridge, he began moaning. I thought it was perhaps for joy, but then I noticed he was looking a touch green under his fur. Since I'd never seen a green dog before, I figured it was just a reflection from the lush hills surrounding us. Then he threw up all over the back seat and I figured otherwise.

The rest of the trip went smoothly, except for trying to find a dog-friendly hotel for four hours. At midnight we ended up sneaking into a Best Western which prominently displayed an "Absolutely NO Pets" sign on its front door. I came up with a line or two in case we got caught: "He's not a pet, Ms. Manager, he's family!" Or "He's my guide dog," although I knew that wouldn't really work, since Joe tended to pull me around as if he were a rabid tow truck.

The next morning, we set out early, so as not to get caught, but we got caught anyway. The manager stared at us imposingly, but chuckled when I offered excuse number one. "That's okay. Just don't let the rest of the people see you. People can be weird about dogs," she said and offered for us to join her family that evening for dinner. "Not many places around here allow dogs for supper." That night she treated us to one of the best on-the-road meals I'd ever eaten. Joe got to lick the plates. He was in dog heaven.

Since that first excursion several years ago, Joe has accompanied me on most of my road trips. Through thick and thin, he's been the best buddy a traveler could have. He was there for the flat tire in the middle of the Mojave Desert at high noon. He was my faithful companion when I got stuck in a blizzard in the Sierra Nevada mountains and had to trudge three miles to the next town on a deserted road. He has shared buggy rides, train rides, ferry rides, old log cabins, fancy hotel rooms, gourmet meals at grand restaurants, and magnificent romps on white sand beaches under the full moon. One day while on a hike, Joe even introduced me to my husband.

Joe had quickly become almost a necessary part of my adventuring. Traveling without him left me feeling as though I'd left part of myself behind. Of course, his genetic propensity for Whizdom did occasionally rear its curly head. In one afternoon I'd rather forget, he performed two separate leg lifts on the same meter maid. And he once chased a raccoon so far into the woods that he ended up in the arms of a family that looked as though they'd just as soon eat a dog as pet one. I had to buy them two buckets of fried chicken to get Joe back.

With all our journeying, something odd was happening to my

senses. I was beginning to notice things I'd never noticed, and to appreciate tiny details that had escaped me for decades. My senses were becoming fine tuned—almost like Joe's. It was a little daunting gaining a dog's-eye view of the world, and I was suddenly glad that Harvey, our pet mouse, hadn't been my longtime traveling buddy.

On our walks, I began to see heretofore invisible life, from tiny insects to far-off deer. Driving past a freshly fertilized field in the Central Valley strangely became a blissful experience. Joe's ecstasy at smelling the manure was contagious, and I'd find myself slowing down, rather than accelerating to get past the pungent aroma. A breeze blowing in from the Pacific was no longer just a breeze. As I watched Joe's nose inspecting every facet of the wind as if it were a rare and delicate flower, it dawned on me how much more there is to this world than what we see as humans.

We began hitting the road for no particular reason. One of the greatest joys of traveling with a dog, I came to realize, is that the destination isn't terribly important. It's the journey that counts. It was somewhat humbling to be taught one of life's greatest lessons by a 65-pound dog with bad breath. But I finally began to understand the mysterious twinkle in Zoe's eyes when she talked of traveling with Whiz.

Cousin Whiz died last year, at the respectable Airedale age of fifteen. He died in his sleep at Zoe's feet somewhere between Cape Cod and Providence. For a while Ed and Zoe stopped traveling, settled in a Connecticut RV park, and started feeling old. But then a poodle-terrier combo wandered into their lives and took a liking to the passenger seat of the RV. They named him Charlie, although they call him "Jerry" in front of Zoe's brother. "He's as good a traveler as they come," beams Ed. "He even got us a free dinner at this Frency place outside Chicago. What a dog."

When Ed and Zoe heard about the gathering of stories for *Travelers' Tales: A Dog's World,* they decided to write a story about Whiz and Charlie. But one day, while trying to dust, uncrust, and de-rust their old IBM Selectric, they decided to chuck the whole idea of writing anything and keep traveling. "I'd rather read stories about dogs traveling than have to settle down and write about 'em. You tell me when that book comes out," said Zoe.

Ed and Zoe, it's out. And it's brilliant, funny, touching, and even inspirational.

Dogs who have to stay at home while their people explore the world outside their front door are going to want to rush out and buy this book. Joe would like to point out some particularly intrepid traveling dogs, such as Sam, who sailed 6,000 miles while just a pup ("Sailing with Sam") and Buddy, whose travels and travails in our hometown of San Francisco ("The Ruff Guide") are reminiscent of our own experiences on the road. The stories in this book show that no matter where you are with a dog, your view of life is going to be significantly different—and usually better—than if you were there without the company of a canine.

These days, dogs inspect Joe with great reverence, and he stands straighter and prouder and puffs up ever so slightly with each sniff. If I happen to know the dog's person, after a couple of visits I'll inevitably get a phone call. "Thanks to you and your dog, we've bowed to Chester's begging. We're taking him on our vacation next week. I don't know why, but we'll give it a try."

At that moment I know that with any luck, a wise dog is soon going to become a very happy dog. And a happy traveler is going to become a little happier, and maybe even a little wiser.

Maria Goodavage is author of The California Dog Lover's Companion, The Bay Area Dog Lover's Companion, *and series editor of* The Dog Lover's Companion *national travel series. She lives in San Francisco with her husband and three children (two of whom have fur).*

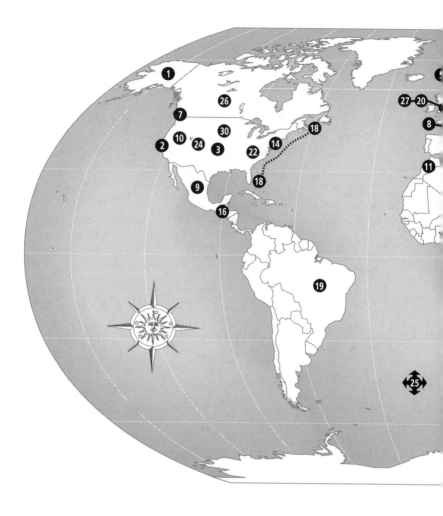

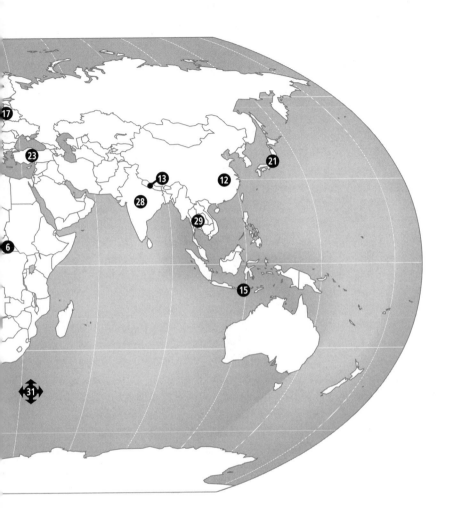

PART ONE

TRAVELING TAILS

GARY PAULSEN

Eagle River

A disastrous start nearly finishes a first run
of "The Last Great Race."

THE PROCESS OF BEGINNING THE IDITAROD IN DOWNTOWN
Anchorage is so insane and so completely out of context with
what the race really represents that it's almost otherworldly. Then,
too, it is all phony—the whole Anchorage start is for television and
audiences and sponsors. The truth is, you cannot run a dog team
from Anchorage to Nome because outside of Anchorage there is
a freeway system that cannot be
stopped, even for something as
intrinsically Alaskan as the
Iditarod. The start is a theatrical
event, and is treated as such by
everybody.

Except the dogs.

And therein lay the problem
of the start. There was much
hoopla, television cameras,
crowds of people, and nearly
fourteen hundred dogs jammed

he Iditarod covers the
1,049 miles between
Anchorage and Nome, Alaska,
and commemorates the 1925 race
against time to provide diphtheria
serum to dying patients. Although
twenty dog teams participated in
the Great Race of Mercy, just one
dog got the statue, book, and
movie—Balto.

—CH

into a short stretch of Fourth Street in the middle of the downtown section. Starting well before the race crowds gathered, loud-

3

speakers began blaring, and dogs started barking as they were harnessed. Barking dogs begot barking dogs and soon the whole street
was immersed in a cacophonous roar that made it impossible to
hear anything.

Worse, the dogs became excited. And like the barking, excitement breeds on itself until dogs I thought I'd known for years were
completely unrecognizable, were almost mad with eagerness. It
wasn't just that they wanted to run—there wasn't anything else for
them. Everything they were, all the ages since their time began, the
instincts of countless eons of wolves coursing after herds of bison
and caribou were still there, caught in genetic strands, and they
came to the fore and the dogs were berserk with it.

And at least as important was that the madness was infectious,
carried to the people, the handlers, the mushers—especially the
rookies. No matter the plan, no matter the words of caution during briefings, what might start sensibly began to pick up speed and
soon everything was imbued with a frantic sense of urgency.
People who walked start to trot, then run, with dogs dragging
them from trucks to get hooked into the gangline to get them
ready to be taken up to the chutes.

By this time I, too, was gone, caught up in the madness of it all,
so immersed in the noise and insanity that if somebody had asked
my name I would not have known it. I could see only the dogs,
lunging on their picket chains, crazed with excitement; feel only
that same pull tearing at me, the power of it all sweeping me.

And there was a very real danger in that power, the unleashed
power of fifteen dogs in prime, perfect condition suddenly being
released in front of a light sled and slick plastic runners. People
would be hurt; people would scratch from the race in the first five
blocks with broken legs, shoulders, collarbones, concussions. Sleds
would be shattered, turned into kindling, and mushers would be
dragged for blocks until bystanders could grab the dogs and stop
them. The power was enormous and could not be controlled.
There were only two inches of snow on the street, trucked in for
the start, and the sleds could not be steered or slowed; brakes
would not work; snowhooks would bounce off the asphalt.

It was here that I began making rookie mistakes, two of which would prove critical to the beginning of the Iditarod for me.

Caught up in anxiety, not wishing to cause problems with the race, I harnessed my dogs too soon, way too soon, and tied the sled off to the bumper of the truck. The difficulty with this was that I had pulled number thirty-two and with the dogs tied on the side, harnessed, and ready to go, waiting to do, crazy to go—every team going up to the chutes had to be taken past my team—they had to wait. Dogs do not wait well. An old Inuit belief states that dogs and white men stem from the same roots because they cannot wait, have no patience, and become frustrated easily, and it showed mightily then.

It took two minutes per team to get them in the chutes, counted down and gone, so there was an hour delay waiting for my team to be called; an hour of slamming into harness, screaming with madness every time a team was taken past us, an hour of frustration and anxiety, an hour that seemed a day, a year.

When finally it was done, or nearly done, and the dogs were complete beyond reason and only three teams were ahead of us, six minutes before chute time, right then I made the second mistake.

I changed leaders. I had Cookie in single lead position. We had worked together for two years and she knew how to lead incredibly well and I trusted her completely. But…

The pre-race jim-jams took me and I started thinking of what I perceived to be reality. I had never raced before and Cookie had never raced, had never led a big team in such confusion. I began to worry that since it was all so new she would not know what to do, would not know how to get out of the chutes and line the team out down the street, would be confused about running a race.

I had a dog that was given to me just before leaving Minnesota. His name was Wilson and I had been told that he had been in races, led in races. (I found out later it was one impromptu race, with a very small team—one dog—and it was only around a yard pulling a child.)

In microseconds the anxiousness about Cookie grew to a mountain and I could easily imagine her being released, stopping in her addled state, getting run over by the team or running into the crowd, heading off in the wrong direction—all I could see was disaster.

With less than three minutes to go I unhooked Cookie and dropped her back to point position (just to the rear of the leader) and put Wilson in the front. This all took moments and before I could think on it, wonder if I'd done the right thing, eleven or twelve volunteers came with a man who was holding a clipboard.

He noted the number of my bib, smiled and nodded. "You're next."

And volunteers took the gangline in back of each set of dogs; I unhooked them from the truck and we surged forward, the dogs nearly dragging the volunteers off their feet as we threaded into the chutes.

People talked to me. A man leaned over and said something and I nodded and smiled but I could not hear a thing over the din from the team. I also had a new sensation. Stark goddamn terror was taking me as I looked down the street over fifteen dogs and realized that this was it, that they were going to take me out hanging like an idiot on the sled.

A man leaned down with a megaphone next to my ear.
"Five!"
"Four!"
"Three!"
"Two!"
"One!"

But the dogs had watched too long, had memorized the count, and when the counter hit three and the volunteers released the team and stood off to the side they lunged, snapped loose from the men holding back the sled and I was, quite literally, gone.

I had started the Iditarod illegally—two seconds too soon.

I do not hold the record for the person coming to disaster soonest in the Iditarod. There have been some mushers who have never left the chutes. Their dogs dove into the spectators or turned back on the team and tried to go out of the chutes backwards. But I rank close.

There is a newspaper photo somewhere showing me leaving the chutes, that shows Wilson with his tongue out the side of his mouth and a wild look in his eye as he snakes the team out and away from the starting line with a great bound. (It also shows me apparently smiling; for the record the smile is not humor but the first stages of rictus caused by something close to terminal fright.)

We made almost two blocks. The distance before the first turn. Wilson ran true down the track left by the previous thirty-one teams. Until the turn. At the end of two blocks there was a hard turn to the right to head down a side street, then out of town on back trails and alleys and into the trees along the highways away from Anchorage.

*W*eeks before the race mushers must send out sacks of food and supplies for distribution along the route and these may only be collected at checkpoints. The average racer will require 2,500 pounds of dog food and at least 1,000 booties for the race. Most checkpoints are in villages where hospitality is available, a few are just crude shelters, but each has a vet who casts an eye over the dogs, offers free advice, medicines, vitamin injections, and can, if necessary, order a dog to be retired.

—Alastair Scott, *Tracks Across Alaska: A Dog Sled Journey*

I remember watching the turn coming at alarming speed. All the dogs were running wide open and I thought that the only way to make it was to lean well to the right, my weight far out to the side to keep the sled from tumbling and rolling.

I prepared, leaned out and into the turn and would have been fine except that Wilson did not take the turn. He kept going straight, blew on through the crowd and headed off into Anchorage on his own tour of discovery.

I could not stop them. The sled brakes and snowhook merely scraped and bounced off the asphalt and concrete. I tried setting the hook in a car bumper as we passed, tearing it off the car (why in god's name are they all made of plastic?), and for a space of either six blocks or six miles—at our speed time and distance became irrelevant—I just hung on and prayed, screaming "WHOA!" every time I caught my breath. Since I had never used the command on the team before it had no effect whatsoever and so I got a Wilson-guided tour of Anchorage.

We went through people's yards, ripped down fences, knocked over garbage cans. At one point I found myself going through a carport and across a backyard with fifteen dogs and a fully loaded Iditarod sled. A woman standing over the kitchen sink looked out with wide eyes as we passed through her yard and I snapped a wave at her before clawing the handlebar again to hang on while we tore down her picket fence when Wilson tried to thread through a hole not much bigger than a housecat. And there is a cocker spaniel who will never come into his backyard again. He heard us coming and turned to bark just as the entire team ran over him; I flipped one of the runners up to just miss his back and we were gone, leaving him standing facing the wrong way barking at whatever it was that had hit him.

I heard later that at the banquet some people had been speaking of me and I was unofficially voted the least likely to get out of Anchorage. Bets were made on how soon I would crash and burn. Two blocks, three. Some said one. It was very nearly true.

Back on the streets I started hooking signs with the snowhook. They were flimsy and bent when the hook hit them and I despaired of ever stopping, but at last my luck turned and the hook caught on a stop sign just right and hung and held the team while I put Cookie back in the lead and moved Wilson— still grinning wildly and snorting steam and ready to rip—back into the team.

I now had control but was completely lost and found myself in the dubious position of having to stop along the street and ask gawking bystanders if they knew the way to the Iditarod trail.

"Well, hell, sure I do. You take this street down four blocks, then cross by the small metal culvert and catch the walking path through the park there until you see the gas station with the old Ford parked out front where you hang a kind of oblique right…"

It is a miracle that I ever got out of town. Finally I reasoned that I had fallen somehow north of the trail and I headed in a southerly direction and when we had gone a mile or so Cookie put her nose down and suddenly hung a left into some trees, around a sharp turn and I saw sled runner marks and we were back on the trail. (As we moved into the small stand of birch and spruce I saw shattered remnants of a sled in the trees and found later that a man had cracked the whip on the turn and hit the trees and broken his leg and had to scratch. He was not the first one to scratch; there had already been two others who gave it up before getting out of town.)

I was four and a half hours getting to the first official check-point at Eagle River—a suburb of Anchorage—where I was met by the handlers and Ruth. We had to unhook the dogs and put them in the truck and drive on the freeway to where the race truly starts, at Knik, on the edge of the bush.

"How's it going?" Ruth asked as I loaded the dogs.

"After this it ought to be all downhill," I said. "Nothing can be as hard as getting out of town…"

It was a statement I would come to think of many times during the following weeks.

Gary Paulsen is one of America's most popular writers for young people and adults alike. This story was excerpted from Winterdance: The Fine Madness of Running the Iditarod, *which, like many of his books, draws upon his vast real-life experience with dogs. He and his wife, painter Ruth Wright Paulsen, live in New Mexico.*

✳

The exhausting 1995 Iditarod was almost over for musher Jeff King. He was only 120 miles from Nome's finish line. As the 1993 champ hustled his disciplined dog team along the trail several miles outside of Elim, a big galumph of a puppy—all paws and floppy ears—started chasing King's sled.

King found out later the pup belonged to the Kalerak family in Elim. Apparently the excitement of hundreds of racing sled dogs sweeping through the tiny Norton Bay village was just too much for the young dog. He ran away to join the fun, and King just happened to be the lucky musher. "He was comically cheering us on," King remembers. "The dog acted a little like an animated cartoon character, tried to pull my mittens off. I tried to shoo him away."

But the situation wasn't funny at the time. It could have meant disqualification for King. "One of my concerns was that [spotter] planes flying over might think I had an injured dog or that I had left Elim with one more dog."

Once, when King stopped the team to adjust something on one of his dogs, he turned around and found the puppy sitting in his sled wagging its tail.

"I finally threw up my arms," King says. The musher tucked the hitch-hiker into the sled bag and kept going. "I was concerned the dog would get too far from home," King says. "I knew somebody cared about him."

By the time they pulled into the next checkpoint at Golovin, the brazen pup had grown on King. He turned the puppy over to race officials, then found out who owned it. He sent a message to Elim that if the Kaleraks were willing to give up the dog, he'd like to keep him. Leaving the dog in Golovin, King took off for White Mountain, where he found a reply from the Kaleraks waiting for him. If King wanted the puppy, it was his.

—Catherine Stadem, "Loose Puppy Adopts Jeff King," *Alaska Magazine*

BRIAN ALEXANDER

The Ruff Guide

*It isn't always cheap or convenient to take
your dog along, but sometimes
it's the only way to go.*

JUDGING FROM THE TERRIFIED LOOK IN HIS EYES, MY DOG, BUDDY, was convinced that travel with his master was a bad idea. Perhaps it was the way the cab driver in San Francisco reenacted the chase scene from *Bullitt*. Perhaps it was the way the driver leaned over the seat, swore at the dog in Arabic, and told me to "keep that dog under control" when Buddy's nose smashed into the driver's head after a particularly violent reunion with terra firma. "Sorry," the driver said later, not really apologizing as I forked over cash, "but in my culture we do not like dogs. In yours it is different, no?"

I looked at Buddy who stood out on the sidewalk wagging his tail with relief, and recalled how he had barfed on the carpet of our hotel room, suffered diarrhea on a lamppost in Union Square, gotten me kicked out of the Fairmont Hotel, denied me access to San Francisco's cable cars, and cost me several hundred dollars in extra travel expense. "No," I answered.

At least not as a travel companion. Buddy, my Alaskan husky, my noble beast of the north, is a sissy. He weeps openly at the sight of ponies. When left alone or in the company of strangers he is as un-abashed in his grief as the mother of the groom at an Irish Catholic wedding. Usually this is merely annoying, but a recent

11

pancreas malfunction left him underweight. And, since Buddy barely eats when left behind, I decided not to risk a starving dog. Hence his presence in San Francisco.

I had been lulled into taking him there by a trip to British Columbia a week earlier. Traveling with Buddy to Victoria seemed simple. I was proud of myself and of Buddy. So when a surprise business trip to San Francisco popped up and Buddy had still not gained enough weight to leave at home, I did not hesitate to say "yes" and book passage for the two of us.

I called United's Shuttle, made reservations and, almost as an afterthought, mentioned I'd be bringing the dog. I was told I would need a kennel, a recent vaccination certificate, and $100 each way for the dog's passage.

"Why?" I asked. "He's not even excess baggage."

"Special handling."

My vet suggested that a drugged in-flight Buddy would be a happier Buddy, so he prescribed a bottle of doggie downers called Acepromizine. Next I stopped into a pet warehouse store with Buddy and inquired about kennels. The saleswoman recommended a large one. I opened the kennel door. Buddy walked in, laid down, refused to leave.

Since I live far enough away from the airport to make early morning flights an experiment in sleep deprivation, I decided to check into a motel near the terminal, a Super 8. The motel was happy to have the dog as long as I paid a $25 deposit in case of doggie damage. "I've been working here three years and we've never had to keep the deposit," the desk clerk said.

As I was signing in, I remembered that I had neglected to tell the Fairmont Hotel in San Francisco, where I had reserved a room, that Buddy would be joining me. But since hotel and motel policy seemed so uniform—some version of deposit or extra charges to cover cleaning costs—I wasn't worried. And besides, in the Super 8, Buddy proved once again that huskies are fastidious dogs. The $25 was returned when I checked out.

The following morning I popped a pill into Buddy and took a

shuttle bus from the motel to the terminal. The driver welcomed the dog with open arms, but dropped us far from the terminal curb. I was forced to rent a luggage cart, find an elevator to the ticketing level, and walk with Buddy to the curbside check in, where, I had been told by the telephone reservations agent, I could check Buddy. It was an hour before flight time.

"You can't check that dog here," the skycap informed me after I had waited in line. "You gotta go inside."

Inside was a line snaking through all the twists in United's roped line-up area, down the terminal hallway and into the next airline's counter space. Buddy and I took up residence.

Finally, half an hour before takeoff, a ticket agent made an announcement for those hoping to board the flight to San Francisco. "Please come down to this area of the counter," she said motioning with her arms. "And please hurry."

Make sure your dog's crate has at least one water dish that hooks onto the door; ground personnel will fill them if they can see them. I write my dog's name on the top of the door of the crate. Many ramp workers will use their names, easing the stress. On the top of the crate I tape a manila folder with a copy of the dog's health certificate. On the outside, I write the address where we're going, local contact number, and return address and phone number.

—Brenda Kivela,
"Travel Pointers," *DogGone*

The agent inspected Buddy's kennel, checked off a list of required accouterments, plastered "Live Animal" and "Up" arrow stickers all over the cage, and a now-groggy Buddy stumbled in and laid down. Easy as pie.

Skis, surfboards, and dogs in kennels are delivered to the odd-size baggage ramp near most airport luggage carousels. In San Francisco, I waited patiently for Buddy, who, I suspected, was still dreaming of Lassie in the sky with diamonds. But a baggage handler rolled up the door to the ramp, threw back the vinyl curtains of his luggage cart and revealed Buddy's kennel, flipped over, with Buddy trembling inside.

"What the hell is this?" I asked.

"No other bags in the cart to stop him from flipping over when I stop quickly," he replied over his shoulder. The idea of not stopping quickly seemed to have escaped him. This was special handling.

Normally, I would have taken the shuttle bus into the city for $8, but dogs are forbidden to ride them, so my only recourse was a cab. Luckily, a station wagon was first in the taxi line, so it easily accommodated dog, kennel, baggage, and me. The driver schmoozed with Buddy in Russian.

The employee at the Fairmont did not schmooze. "I think you're gonna have a problem with this dog," he said. "I don't think we take 'em." Traffic backed up in the Fairmont's driveway as I discussed options with the employee.

"Listen," he said, "I know a side door…"

"I'm not paying $250 a night to sneak in and out of a side door," I declared proudly. The bellman stood patiently by the kennel. Traffic backed into Mason Street.

"Okay, okay," he said conspiratorially. "Listen, tell them he's a seeing eye dog. They take seeing eye dogs." I considered sunglasses, but I imagined Buddy leading me directly into one of the Fairmont's marble pillars.

I walked into the lobby, strode confidently to the front desk, announced my name to Sonja, the clerk, who promptly produced my paperwork. "Oh, and I have my dog with me," I said casually as I filled out the form.

"I'm sorry, you cannot keep a dog in the room," Sonja responded.

"Well, he's standing outside," I said, hoping she would take this as *fait accompli*.

"We have a very strict policy. No dogs."

"Umm, he's a guide dog," I said. "He's in training. He's learning."

Sonja dashed through a door behind the front desk and returned with reinforcements in the form of the day manager. "Your dog is a guide dog?" the manager asked incredulously. I thought of Buddy's bad pancreas, his weeping, his habit of tripping over stairs.

"I'm hoping he makes the team. He's in training."

"But you do not depend on him."

I admitted as much, then reached into my pocket, took out all the cash I had, and said, "Look, I'll, you know, pay a deposit. In cash." They both stared at me, clearly unaware of when they were being bribed. I winked. "I could pay it now. Some extra charge, maybe?"

"Ahh, man, you blew it," the employee said as, now homeless, I sat next to Buddy on the front steps of the hotel. "I coulda gotten you in, man!"

A taxi was quickly summoned, the kennel loaded, and, as we drove away, I thought I could hear the Fairmont breathe a sigh of relief.

Hotels it turns out, vary considerably on their pet policies. Some take animals, some require deposits or extra fees, and some flatly refuse entry. Policies differ even within chains. Some Ritz-Carltons take dogs, some do not. Some Hiltons do, some do not. Some Holiday Inns do, some do not.

Fortunately, the St. Francis, a Westin property, does. (Most Westins prefer a 25-pound limit on dogs, but rarely turn away a guest with a larger dog unless it appears to be ill behaved.) The front desk welcomed the dog, and gave us a view room on the 28th floor of the hotel's modern tower section. Nice for me, bad for the dog. Buddy decided a glass elevator with no visible means of support running up the exterior of a building was a bad idea. I had to drag him into it.

Staff and guests alike fussed over Buddy. Cable car drivers did not. Without a muzzle, Buddy was canine *non grata*. So we walked. Restaurants denied us entry and with no car in which to place the

The Four Seasons Boston does not set aside certain rooms for guests with pets but rather deep-cleans the room after the pet's departure. In the rooms they provide their pet guests with a pet bed, dry food, and water. Also available is a special Pet Menu which offers such items as grilled chicken and fresh corn for dogs and poached salmon with steamed rice for cats.

—Fran Golden,
"A Four-Paws Review"

dog, I found myself waiting by parking meters as cafés prepared carry-out dinners.

I could have contacted the Society for Prevention of Cruelty to Animals in San Francisco which operates a Doggie Day Care center, but the center is fifteen minutes by taxi from Union Square. A center worker very graciously volunteered to come to the hotel and sit with the dog at night so I could go out, but I felt guilty asking a stranger to baby-sit my dog. The hotel recommended a baby-sitting service that charged $8 per hour for a four-hour minimum and a $20 referral fee to sit a dog. I chose to save the $52.

This was a mistake. Buddy, who was still hardly eating, showed such an interest in my carry out veal-stuffed tortellini in cream sauce, that I allowed him to finish my leftovers. He gobbled them in a flash.

The next day, however, as I sat working at the desk in my room, Buddy calmly stood up, spread his legs, and resurrected the pasta. I cleaned the small spot immediately and completely. Buddy lay down. I began typing. Buddy stood up. He paced. He looked at the door. He looked at me. He looked at the door. He howled.

I grabbed his leash, dashed out the door, and dragged him into the elevator. Buddy and I raced through the lobby at a pace I prayed would avoid general panic. As soon as we hit the grass of Union Square, Buddy unfolded his *National Geographic*. I had given my dog Montezuma's revenge. On the bright side, I had taken him behind some palm trees. Nobody was taking notice. I could escape without scooping. But when Buddy was hit by a cramp, he released a bloodcurdling howl straight from his genetic cousins in the wild. About a thousand people in downtown San Francisco turned to watch my dog defecate on a historic lamppost.

I placed Buddy on a food fast and there were no more bowel incidents. Still, I breathed a sigh of relief when we walked into San Francisco International. After giving him a pill, I delivered his kennel to the odd-sized baggage counter and happily retreated to my gate.

"Is passenger Brian Alexander in the boarding area?"

There was, the gate agent said, a problem with my dog. Back at odd-sized baggage, a man whose job is loading the bellies of air-planes had decided Buddy's kennel was cruel. Feeding my dog veal-stuffed tortellini in cream sauce was cruel. Making him ride with a crazed taxi driver may have been cruel. Buddy's kennel was certainly not cruel.

"He's gotta be able to stand fully upright in the kennel," the baggage handler said. "The SPCA is at airports inspecting, this does not meet specs. You can't fly him. I won't load him."

I later learned that a brochure from the Air Travel Association says the kennel should indeed be large enough for the animal to fully stand up and should have a small water and food dish. The animal should be eight weeks old, have a vet's certificate of good health issued no more than ten days before departure, be accli-mated to temperatures below 45 degrees when such conditions exist, and not be drugged unless a vet says okay. But no matter how cushy the animals accommodations, the ATA says "advance arrange-ments are not guarantees that your animal will travel on a specific flight...airlines reserve the right to refuse to handle an animal..." This is further complicated by the conflicting information airlines reservations agents give out.

American Airlines said a dog need not stand fully upright as long as it was comfortable. Delta said nothing about needing a health certificate or about kennel size, though it did say it offers approved kennels for sale at its ticket counters. Neither Delta nor United mentioned the requirement for including a small water and food dish. All agreed lap-sized dogs whose kennels could fit under a seat could fly in the cabin. None mentioned the required stick-ers. All charged $100 each way within the continental U.S.

At the moment, though, I knew none of this. I was angry. I protested that half a dozen United employees had already handled Buddy's kennel. I told him about the kennel being flipped upon arrival and that his concern might be misplaced. Our voices rose.

"Hey, your dog's shaking in there," he said accusingly.

"Of course the dog is shaking!" I shouted. "You hauled him out there, brought him back, and now we're arguing. He was sleeping when I left!"

"The dog's gotta be able to turn around in his kennel."

I let Buddy out. He licked my face. I gritted my teeth and shoved a now-reluctant Buddy back in head first. He promptly turned around. The employees huddled. "I've seen dogs that size go out of here in kennels a lot smaller than that," one said. I won. "But next time ask us first, we make the decisions," the handler said self-importantly. I asked him to give me his phone number so I could call him directly next time. He did not think this was funny.

In the end, Buddy and I arrived home safe and sound, but I think our days as travel companions are over. I found a flyer on— no kidding—"Canine Separation Anxiety" at my vet's. I called the number. Buddy has been signed up for puppy Prozac.

Brian Alexander is the author of Green Cathedrals: A Wayward Traveler in the Rain Forest *and the editor of the forthcoming* Travelers' Tales Greece. *He is currently training Buddy to sit in business class.*

★

We were frequent guests at the Holiday Inn National Airport in Crystal City, Virginia, and all the staff there knew us by sight. They also knew our 120-pound Great Dane, Shana, by name.

It seems that hotel crime was suddenly reduced whenever we were conspicuously in the hotel, and that is probably one reason the staff always seems glad to see us arrive. The manager would occasionally walk with us through part of the lobby and bar area, and I once heard him tell some people, "This dog is always here." I suppose no one wanted to see if she could switch into "Guard Dog Mode."

One occasion, during Ronald Reagan's second inauguration, we were sent to Washington on very short notice. I called our hotel, the Holiday Inn, and gave them my usual greeting, "Hello, this is Emmett Black with General Electric...." but the response was "I'm sorry sir. We've been booked up for months." So I called every other hotel in the area and got pretty much the same response.

With sudden inspiration, or perhaps desperation, I called back the Holiday Inn. This time I said, "Hello, this is Shana's human...." and this time the response was, "Oh, yes sir. Come on down. We always have a room for you."

It seemed that the staff knew Shana's name, but didn't know mine. It really puts you in your place when your dog can get a hotel room, but you can't.

—J. Emmett Black. Jr., "Shana"

MELISSA A. PRIBLO CHAPMAN

Cross-Country Dog

*A life-long dream comes true—and yields
a number of surprises for a young woman
on horseback with her dog.*

ONCE IN A WHILE, WHEN YOU HAVE A DREAM, CIRCUMSTANCES come together and seem to say, "Now is your chance." Since childhood, my dream had been to ride horseback—alone—across the United States. My chance came when I was 23 years old.

I owned a strong healthy horse called Raindance and had spent the previous couple of years studying maps, conditioning my horse, and saving a little money. We had taken practice camping trips and accumulated the proper equipment. That spring everything had fallen into place. There was no reason not to try.

As the planned departure date drew nearer and most of my preparations were complete, something seemed to be missing. This feeling intensified during the trial runs when Raindance and I would camp alone. I love my horse; he is affectionate and has plenty of personality. But there is nothing like a dog to fill the void when I don't really need another human voice but I don't want to be completely alone either.

As a lifelong dog lover, though, I felt torn; would I be jeopardizing the safety of a dog by taking it with me? Was it selfish asking a dog to endure the extremes of weather, traffic, and terrain, and the unknown risks I could encounter, and to stay obediently by my side during all of it? Oh yes, and learn to ride a horse, too.

Despite these concerns, my sister and I (she was to be the objective voice) began looking for the "right" dog. We saw many breeds and possibilities but something always held me back. Then one day we were won over by a mixed-breed pup at a local dog shelter. Her intelligent and expressive face touched me, yet I went home without her, still plagued with doubt. I could not forget her, though, and several days later I awoke with a sudden start, knowing I had to have that dog. I drove to the shelter hurriedly, praying she would still be there. She was—looking as if she expected me. I knew it was fate that we found each other.

So I added in dog conditioning and training those last few months before we left. The unique training that this puppy (soon appropriately named Gypsy) required was built on a foundation of basic obedience techniques, with variations to suit our special needs. Since she was always by my side, she learned to heel quickly and easily. At first, I rode Rainy with Gypsy tucked inside my winter coat, only her head peering out curiously. Eventually I began to set her down behind Rainy and repeat the heel command. Her collie-shepherd background helped; she seemed to know instinctively how to act around livestock, and fell naturally into place behind Raindance on the trail. Rainy, for his part, was extremely tolerant of our new companion. He even stood still for her when she later taught herself to jump right up in the saddle.

By spring of that year, it was time to see if we could really make this dream come true. We were as ready as possible. On May 1st, I said good-bye to my worried friends and family, and my horse and dog and I set out in upstate New York, heading for California.

Oh, how different from my fantasies the reality of life on the road proved to be. It was quite a big adjustment to go from a happy comfortable life to being without human companionship, not knowing what the next day or the next mile held in store for us. After a few days of sunburn, rain, mosquitoes, and homesickness, the thought of how far we really had to go would enter my thoughts, making our task seem almost insurmountable. Life on the road runs through the gamut of situations and emotions. In some places we were treated like heroes, and in some, we were just alone, finding the safest place to spend the night. Whichever it was though, Gypsy was a comforting presence, and she never left my side. Once we were guests at a luxurious home where Gypsy and I slept on a waterbed. The very next night we found ourselves camping in an old abandoned barn. I had set the sleeping bag on the floor, but after hearing things crawling around, I moved it up on a picnic table being stored in there. Without a moment's hesitation, Gypsy climbed right up on that picnic table and curled up, as if it were perfectly normal to travel on horseback all day and place ourselves in extremely different situations each night. Gypsy's merry spirit never wavered, no matter what, and before too long, after the initial adjustment period, this became a way of life for all three of us.

D ogs are…wonderful. Truly. To know them and to be with them is an experience that transcends—a way to understand the joyfulness of living and devotion.

—Gary Paulsen, *Winterdance: The Fine Madness of Running the Iditarod*

I learned to delight in the simple pleasures. While the rest of the world was working, I was spending my days out in the open, breathing in the scents of fresh mown grass and evergreens. We made our way slowly but surely, accompanied by the song of roadside streams and the clip clop of Raindance's hooves. I grew to appreciate deeply that I lived with my beloved dog and horse, in a life of my own choosing, with no watch and no calendar. I was free. I learned to take each day and each mile one at a time. As for Gypsy, really, what better life could a dog ask for? She was with me twenty-four hours a day. We ate together, slept together, and grew dependent on each other, horse, dog, and I, in a way that is hard to define. It was just the three of us, every day, together.

When we'd made it far enough to attract media attention, reporters often asked me what I would do if Raindance were injured: would I get another horse and go on? The answer was no. They were always surprised when I said the same was true of Gypsy, too. It was hard to explain that the gangly young pup was as integral a part of the journey as the horse who carried us.

Freedom and adventure carry a price tag; sometimes it's lonely and sometimes it's dangerous. Gypsy was the one who kept the loneliness and homesickness at bay on those nights when the rain poured down on our tent and no one in the whole world knew where we were. She was the one who made me laugh by grabbing the hat off my head and running, and the one who learned to "ham it up" for photographers by holding the reins in her teeth as she sat in the saddle, and to pose proudly like a tourist at landmarks while I took her picture. Gypsy is one of those rare dogs that is liked by everyone, even those who don't ordinarily care for dogs. Once we were the guests at an Amish farm. Since the Amish firmly believed that animals were for working, dogs were never allowed in the house. But after observing us together they knew Gypsy did have a job—to stay with me! And they opened their home to both of us. A woman whose Kansas ranch we visited summed it up when she said, "A dog like that belongs with you. She's family."

Gypsy warmed hearts and opened doors for us across the East and Midwest that summer. Our route took us from the Endless Mountains of Pennsylvania, on through gently rolling farmlands and grassy plains. In Kansas, when we had been on the road over a quarter of a year and were at the approximate halfway point in our journey, Raindance injured his withers. I got him to a vet who said he needed to rest for a few weeks before he'd know if we should go on. Imagine how it felt standing there in a town where I didn't know anyone, and I needed a place to stay with a dog and a horse. It didn't seem possible to have come so far, only to find that our trip might end there. But again fate was watching out for us, for the couple who had helped get us to the vet insisted that we stay with them on their farm while Raindance had a chance to heal. They became like a second family to me. It was with their help that we found Amanda the mini-mule, and added her to our little caravan as a pack animal, to ease the burden on Raindance. Amanda showed me that much of what they say about the nature of mules is true, and she proved it when we started back out again. On the first day after leaving our "second home" she bucked all the packs off and scattered our vital belongings all over the roadside. I climbed off Rainy and began picking up and re-packing. A few minutes into this job, I realized that my precious dog, sensing my dark mood, was picking up what items she could in her mouth and dragging them near to where Amanda was tied.

Though we had frequently been invited into people's homes, after our layover in Kansas—Raindance was completely recovered—we began camping more often in the southwest as towns and ranches became farther apart, and the terrain tougher and more desolate. Together, we waited out a storm huddled in a roadside ditch as lightning crashed around us, and Gypsy once battled a rattlesnake for me in the Panhandle of Texas. It was there, in one of our scariest episodes, that she warned me that a man was approaching the outside of our tent. It turned out all right but it was reassuring to hear that surprising throaty growl come from her. Another time, I had occasion to see that uncanny sensitivity dogs have when we stayed in an old miners' cabin in Arizona. Amid strange thumps and scratches, and a piece of wood falling for no reason, my nervous horses stamped restlessly outside. I still get teased about this, but when Gypsy's hair stood up along her back and she snarled and growled at a corner where I could see nothing, I ran out of there! I watched the sun come up over the brushy landscape from a corral fence nearby, and the animals stayed away from that cabin too. My dream and my perseverance were sorely tested by these trials, but they served to strengthen the bond between my animals and me, and to illustrate to me how deeply I could value the companionship of a dog.

Raindance continued to carry us unerringly across the Continental Divide in New Mexico and the San Francisco Peaks of northern Arizona. Much of the riding we did at that point was on reservation land. Gypsy came into her first heat around this time and occasionally we were followed by a cautious coyote or a free-roaming dog, so I kept Gypsy on the saddle for most of that time. We made one stop at a lonely little general store on the Navajo reservation, and I let Gypsy down long enough to take her post right outside the door while I went in for water and a few supplies. In what seemed like just a moment, I was back outside, but it was, unfortunately, just long enough for a big dog from out of nowhere to have found Gypsy. It was several days ride before I could get anywhere near a vet, so there was no hope of getting her a shot in time. I just had to hope that the breeding wouldn't take.

We kept our steady pace as the summer gave way to a chilly autumn. Eventually we crossed the southern tip of Nevada and into California. After six months and over three thousand miles on the road, what a moment of emotional triumph as we crossed that state line!

The good people of the border towns along the Colorado river—Kingman and Bullhead City, Arizona, and Laughlin, Nevada—arranged for a reception for us as we arrived in the town of Needles, in the California desert. Among the waiting reporters and townspeople, they had set out a table for the celebration with a decorated cake and bottle of champagne for me, two silver buckets full of grain for Rainy and Amanda, and a huge rawhide chew for Gypsy. She once again posed proudly for more pictures, with her prize held firmly in her teeth.

After spending several weeks in California, we began the task of arranging transportation back home. Many people had kept track of us as our journey progressed and piece-by-piece, town-to-town, state-to-state, these animal lovers, friends, and well-wishers with horse trailers got us heading back east again. Stopping in Yates Center, Kansas to visit again with the family who had so kindly taken us in before, I guess Gypsy decided that that was the closest thing to home she had known in her young, well-traveled life. So she calmly walked into the bedroom closet there and began an early delivery of ten (yes, ten) healthy puppies. Fortunately, not one kind soul reneged on the rides home, though I did have to call and let my family know that though I had started out with a horse and a dog, I was returning home with a horse, a dog, a mule, and ten puppies!

My travels across the United States with my dog and horse and mule showed me a perspective of America that few people experience. That trip is a part of my life still, in many ways, as I carry the joy from our adventure inside me. Gypsy, and my horse Raindance, are the wings that gave my dream flight.

Gypsy has been a part of all of the "journeys" of my adult life. She was my roommate in my first apartment, she is in my wedding pictures, she paced with me the first time I felt the early throes of labor, and she was at the door to greet each new baby that joined our home. She lived to be a grand old lady of nearly fifteen, and rode with Raindance and me every day, right up to the week before she died. Her absence now is like a hole in my house and in my heart. So though the wide open spaces and the freedom of the open road are long behind me now, I'm sure that when I am an old, old lady myself, my time together with Gypsy will be among the dearest of my memories. Bless her sweet soul.

Melissa A. Priblo Chapman is a happily married mother of three who continues to share her life with the animals who made her cross-country dream come true. She lives in upstate New York and rides year 'round and in all types of interesting weather. She has had articles published in several national magazines. This story was first published in Good Dog!® *magazine.*

★

I will never forget one day when Cooper and I were training for the walk. It was a boiling August day back in Alfred, the small town in upper New York state where I graduated from college in May of 1973. Cooper and I ran our eleven-mile alternate training route, pacing along an old logging road. I was using the weight of my body to push me down the rock pathway while Cooper stayed a constant three feet from my right calf. Although there were rocks everywhere, my feet and ankles were so hard I didn't have to concentrate of them. Instead, I looked straight ahead, yearning for the river at the bottom of the hill that Cooper and I would swim across.

Suddenly Cooper darted in front of me, nudged me to the side and grabbed a thick copperhead in his mouth. With one vicious, tearing shake, he killed the snake that I would have stepped on and that would have bitten me for sure! This was the first time Cooper saved me, but it wouldn't be the last.

—Peter Jenkins, *A Walk Across America*

Thin Ice

As a 50th birthday present to herself, the author became the first
woman to ski to the magnetic North Pole, accompanied
only by an Inuit husky named Charlie.

THE WIND CONTINUED TO SLACKEN, BUT IT WASN'T UNTIL SIX that I could see far enough ahead to travel safely. A heavy ice fog had developed in the early hours of the morning, but by six had thinned so that visibility was about a quarter of a mile. I had been afraid to leave any sooner. The ice pack was too broken up to risk traveling. But now the wind, our captor, was gone, the doors of our prison had been flung open, and we were free to go.

Charlie appeared more than ready to move on. He had also been restless during the night, getting up and turning in tight circles to make a "nest" before lying down again, curled up in a ball. I was already packed, so after a handful of crackers and walnuts for me and dog food for Charlie we left. The minus fifteen degrees was more comfortable than the lower temperatures of the first few days, but I felt uneasy about it. Did it mean another storm was on the way? And the wind, although now slight, was still from the south, which meant the weather was unsettled enough to bring another storm.

The sun shone thinly through the light ice fog. The blowing now had drifted and was packed tightly into low ridges from a few inches to two feet high. Looking anxiously around for signs of cracks, I saw numerous pencil-thin lines across the ice and several gaps up to three inches across. We arrived at the first of these gaps and Charlie stepped carefully to the edge, looked down at the cold, black water, paused a moment, then stepped nervously across, watching the water beneath him. "It's all right, Charlie," I said, using my most encouraging tone of voice. He obviously didn't like to step across water, but by now he had gained confidence in me and was willing to trust my judgment.

After twenty minutes of careful travel, we came to a particularly fractured area with wide gaps almost three feet across, stretching east to west across our path. I looked down into the inky blackness of the water and shuddered, thinking of what it would be like to fall in. The sudden cold shock would be paralyzing, perhaps fatal. I had visions of the horrible stories I had been told of sled dogs that fell in the water and were cut loose to prevent them from pulling the rest of the team in with them. Sometimes they scrambled out, but if the currents were strong they disappeared under the ice. No wonder Charlie was so cautious around open water. He knew the consequences of falling in.

Looking ahead at the maze of cracks and gaps we would have to find a safe way through, I was struck by a dark thought. If I made a mistake and Charlie or I fell in the water, his trust in me would be for nothing. When we began this journey, he was an Inuit dog, accustomed to a life devoid of human kindness. He learned, as all Inuit dogs do, to be careful around humans. After all, the slightest infraction could at the very least bring a swift kick to the ribs, while a moderate mistake could end in death. Charlie certainly had no reason to trust a human with his life. But he trusted me.

He stood now, leaning lightly against my right leg, waiting for me to decide what to do. He had developed this habit of light contact when he was around open water or was unsure of my next move, and I had learned to give him definite body signals to indicate the plan ahead. His "What do we do next?" reaction was very different from his confident, in-control, protective, go-get-em polar bear stance. As I patted his head he looked up at me, his love and trust showing in his dark eyes. Quickly bending down I hugged him tightly. The thought of any harm coming to Charlie felt like a lead weight on my shoulders. I loved this big, black, furry dog, and somehow we would get through safely to the pole. It was a precious gift to be trusted and loved by a dog that had never learned trust and had never known human kindness.

An Eskimo legend tells of how dogs came over to the side of the humans when a big rift opened up in the earth, separating people from the animals who fled to the other side. Only the dog stood by at the edge of the abyss, begging to be rescued. A man called to the dog and urged it to leap across. The dog leapt, and landing short, hung on by its paws. The man pulled the dog up out of the brink, forever sealing the bond between the two creatures, and thus beginning a working collaboration that for centuries provided transportation to Arctic peoples around the world.

—Barbara Ras,
"April in the Arctic"

Once more I looked ahead at the fractured ice, trying to see a way through without having to go a long way around. I was surprised at the thinness of the ice pack. Only one to two feet thick, it was several feet thinner than the ice we had traveled over the last few days, which explained why it had fractured under the stress of the storm.

All at once the ice began to move again, cracking and grinding in all directions. I stood terrified as the gap in front of me slowly closed to only inches. The winds of the past two days combined with the tides were still moving the ice pack. Quickly taking advantage of the now-narrow split, we stepped over. The next gap, a few yards away, was wider and slowly opening. I grabbed Charlie, urging him to hurry, and we scrambled over that one too. But then there was a sharp bang and a crack raced through the ice just inches in front of my ski tips. My mouth was dry with fear. I wanted out of here and fast. We crossed the new split only to reach the edge of a gap three feet across. I was afraid it would suddenly widen. To allow Charlie to jump without the traces of his sled pulling backward, I quickly attached his sled to a long rope. His head cocked with uncertainty, he watched me approach the crack. My skis, although bending alarmingly in the middle, reached across the gap and I stepped across, pulling my sled over after me.

Poor Charlie felt this was the limit. A few inches were all right, but this? I leaned toward him with my hand outstretched, calling his name, trying to sound calm and confident. After a few moments staring down at the dreaded water, he jumped. His powerful body sailed over gracefully and easily. I patted and fussed over him to show how impressed I was. Looking pleased with himself, he responded to my big hug with a lick across my face, which I interpreted as a kiss. All I had to do now was pull his sled over.

The ice fog was rapidly disappearing, making it easy to see the ice surface ahead. I stopped to listen. The ice was silent again. Perhaps we had experienced its last convulsion. I hoped so. We passed over several more splits and gaps, the widest no more than three feet across. Charlie was doing fine. I had tied his sled behind mine. My pulling his sled made it easier for him to jump across the gaps. He walked at my side, trusting me completely as we wound our way through the fractured ice. After a few more jumps he didn't even hesitate, sometimes even jumping ahead of me. His confidence improved with every leap. I depended on Charlie to warn me of polar bears, while he relied on my confidence to help him cross open water.

Helen Thayer is a professional mountain guide, sled racer, and a U.S. National Luge Champion (1975). In 1992, she and her 65-year-old husband, Bill, became the first—and oldest—married couple to reach the magnetic North Pole on foot, unsupplied. When they are not out breaking records and misconceptions, Helen, Bill, and Charlie live in Washington State. This story was excerpted from her book, Polar Dream: The Heroic Saga of the First Solo Journey by a Woman and Her Dog to the Pole.

✳

Just before halting for lunch we noticed Geoff stopped in the lead, his body prone to the ground in an awkward position. Dahe, one hand firmly grasping the sled, signaled with the other for us to come quickly. As I neared their sled I understood the predicament: Geoff was struggling with a tug line that dropped straight down through the ice, and a dog dangled from the end of it, swinging wildly in a deep crevasse.

Actually three dogs had fallen into the crevasse. Two dangled from their harnesses, but Spinner had fallen out of his and landed on a ledge 25 feet down. Luckily for him he had "chosen" the perfect place to land, because on either side of the narrow sill that held him the blue void widened as it dropped into blackness. We quickly pulled the two harnessed dogs to safety, relieving Geoff's strain, but it took ten long minutes to set up a belay system for Jean-Louis, who would drop into the crevasse and put a spare harness around Spinner, who was frozen in terror.

Once we lowered Jean-Louis down inside the crevasse, he had a hard time getting the harness on the frightened dog in such narrow confines. Once he managed, the pair was pulled to safety quickly. The aftermath—untangling the snarls in the rest of Geoff's team, repacking rescue gear—took an hour.

—Will Steger and Jon Bowermaster, *Crossing Antarctica*

VICKY WINSLOW

Through a Dog's Eyes

A guide dog provides a different point of view
for a young student traveling in Holland.

I SPENT MY LAST CAREFREE SUMMER IN HOLLAND, STUDYING AS A guest of the Dutch government, transported far away from anything familiar and known. The only sure thing was a 50-pound cream-colored yellow Labrador retriever whose job was to guide me around a country neither of us had ever seen. It was her job to see it for us both; to interpret for me the canals, the windmills, and the twisting streets of cities that were old when my country was new. It was my job to interpret for her the many signals coming up to me from her harness, "forward," "right," and "left;" simple directions which she could follow. Her name was Honey and together we explored the bridges and tram lines of Amsterdam.

We made forays into the wide open countryside, to its fields redolent of cows. As Honey and I both inhaled their rich scent, I looked forward to sampling all varieties of cheeses Holland had to offer. Honey's diet, on the other hand, was something which had worried me. I brought no food, due to the customs laws, so one of the first trips I attempted was to a local pet store in search of dog food. Honey had the iron stomach of her breed and I wasn't concerned about the sudden change in diet. But I wanted to find something similar to what she ate at home. On entering the pet store Honey led me to a large cage which contained a parrot whose raucous Dutch was better than the halting phrases I managed to stammer out. With a good-humored but very rudimentary verbal exchange, the proprietor and I settled on a large bag of something which smelled more like horse feed than dog food but which Honey gobbled down happily each day.

My exploration of Amsterdam was marred by only one incident that happened during my first street crossing. As usual, I listened to the flow of traffic, and when I thought it was safe, I gave Honey the "forward" command. We made it easily to the far curb where she halted in the prescribed manner. But as I stood there on what I thought was the sidewalk, the dog beside me became more and more agitated. In trying to decide in which direction I should turn next, I had laid the harness handle down on her back. This was a signal to Honey that my guide was not working. However, instead of calmly waiting for me, her agitation increased the longer we stood there. Eventually, even I heard what she had seen long ago, and quickly I picked up the harness handle and was dragged off the tram tracks and to the real curb as the tram pulled in.

"Sorry about that, girl," I managed. "Nobody told me they had tracks down the middle of the street here."

Honey turned to look at me, and I could feel in her posture the exasperation in her eyes.

As the weeks passed we explored the country together. With Honey leading the way, I climbed the spiral staircases in medieval castles, reaching over my head to hold the harness as she climbed before me. We toured museums and listened to the descriptions of paintings which I would never see nor could Honey ever show me. Still, the works of Van Gogh, Vermeer, and Rembrandt were brought to life for me as I listened to the vivid details of each work.

One day, we were walking along a busy country road on our way to town. As we walked both dog and human were engaged in a silent tug-of-war. I wanted to stay as far to the left as possible, away from the speeding traffic, while all of Honey's instincts told her to keep away from the edge of the road. As the two of us fought, cars honked their horns and their drivers shouted words which I had not yet come across in my Dutch vocabulary book. By the time we reached town, we were both hot and tired, and I decided to stop for a cold drink at one of the small sidewalk cafés which dotted the village. While we cooled off, I resolved that the road we just walked would be off limits for us in the future. When a friend happened by the café, I gladly accepted a ride back.

"I don't see where you could have walked," said my friend on the return trip. "There's absolutely no room for pedestrians, just the road, then a sheer drop on the left into the canal."

Vicky Winslow is a freelance writer living in New York City. She holds a B.A. in English literature from Barnard College, and is currently working with her fourth seeing eye dog.

✳

"Where's the coffee shop?" we wondered. My friend Barbara and I were poring over the two-volume Braille program provided at an American Council of the Blind convention. "It says there's a coffee shop, but it doesn't say where it is."

During that day and the next two, we inquired several times about the coffee shop but no one knew where it was. So accompanied by our seeing eye dogs, we immersed ourselves in the many fun-filled activities planned during our stay in the spacious Chicago hotel.

On the fourth day, however, as we were on our way out of the hotel, we noticed a change. Actually, it was my four-footed guide Hennie who noticed the difference. The door on our right which had been closed until now was open. The turn of Hennie's head caused a slight swivel of her harness, and that let me know there was a room on our right that we could go into. Since we were on our way out, I said, "Hennie, no, forward," and gave her the corresponding hand signal.

Upon our return we started to pass the same location and once more my furry guide indicated the presence of an open door, a possible destination. Ordinarily I do not act upon unsolicited suggestions from Hennie, but this time curiosity got the better of me.

As Barbara and I walked through the door, the welcoming aroma of a familiar hot breakfast beverage greeted us, and we happily ordered gourmet coffee and pastry.

We heard an amiable lady come up to our table and remark, "I kept hoping that your dog would bring you in here each time you went by. We were closed during the Fourth of July weekend and just opened up again this morning."

—Camille T. Petrecca, "A Golden Moment"

ROBERT BURNHAM

Story from the C.A.R.

*Sometimes it's better to let the dog
do the talking.*

SIX HOURS AFTER LEAVING PARIS ON A COLD JANUARY NIGHT, MY wife, Kathy, and I arrived in the Central African Republic. She had lived and worked in the C.A.R. before, but it was something new and amazing for me. Ambling across the tarmac, burdened by my heavy winter coat and oversized carry-on bag, I was amazed by the heat, the humidity, and brightness of the early morning sun. More importantly, going through airport customs and immigration, I immediately learned that my language skills needed an upgrade. In order to enjoy my stay in the C.A.R., I knew that I was going to have to improve my French and learn a bit of the national language, Sango.

A week after our arrival in Bangui, Kathy came home from work and told me that the couple running the Peace Corps transit house had puppies that they were giving away. We had always wanted to have a dog, but we had never had enough room in our small city apartment back home. We went to the transit house right after dinner that evening and a week later we were able to bring Alekum home with us in a small straw basket. He was beautiful, a reddish-brown mix of a boxer with incredibly expressive brown eyes and a playful and rambunctious temperament. Right

37

away, the three of us became inseparable; Alekum became an instant member of our family.

Taking Alekum on an afternoon walk past the soccer stadium and vast empty shell of Bangui's sports arena soon became an integral part of my daily routine. His reddish coat and boxer build made him stand out from the smaller, thinner dogs in our neighborhood, but what really attracted attention was the completely bizarre way that I treated him. The word around the neighborhood was that Alekum's owner, the lanky "*munju*" (white person) who lived in the house by the university, would not just let the dog run on his own, but instead tied a piece of rope around the dog's neck and then walked around town behind him. Bizarre!

The young children who lived in our neighborhood decided that following Alekum and me around on our daily walk would be a great way to pass an hour each afternoon; thus we always had a small handful of young boys following us around town at a cautious distance. Along the way the kids would kick an old rubber ball as if it were a soccer ball, wrestle with each other, call out to other friends passing by, and speculate aloud about Alekum. From what I could understand, they were convinced that Alekum, walking under the hot African sun, had the longest tongue of any dog they had ever seen. The most urgent topic of their discussions, however, was on the subject of whether or not Alekum was a mean dog.

The case for Alekum being a ferocious beast was strong. The kids had all seen his one great dash for freedom, the day he had escaped out of the house and chased a goat around our neighborhood at full speed for fifteen minutes before being lured back inside by promises of an early dinner and a generous assortment of doggie treats. Alekum had created chaos, tipping over buckets of water that had been hand carried from the pump, and sending tens of small children and chickens running for cover. More damning, according to the six-year-old prosecutor presenting his case, was the immediate evidence at hand—the strong piece of rope that I had tied around Alekum's neck and which connected him to my wrist. Why would anyone tie up their dog like this unless he was an extremely vicious and savage animal?

The boy presenting the case for the defense was nervous. His objections had been overturned and his circumstantial evidence had been soundly refuted by the prosecution. He had only one chance to make his case; he had to call me to testify in Alekum's defense. At the turn-around point, halfway through our walk, I was finally confronted by the young boys who wanted a definitive judgment from me. Was, or was not, Alekum a wild lion of a dog? Wasn't it true that he was an incredibly angry and cruel animal? I stopped, translating their words from Sango (which I still really did not understand), and tried to formulate my response concisely.

I smiled and said, "*Lo té zo. Lo té zo mingi!*"

The children's mouths opened and the youngest ones screamed before breaking and running toward home. Alekum, confused by the display, grew alarmed and started barking loudly as the children scattered in front of him. I was also confused, so I re-played in my head what I just told the boys. Then it hit me, I had just substituted the verb *té* (to eat) for *yé* (to like); thus my sentence had been, "He eats people. He eats people a lot!"

Though I tried to correct my statement to the kids many times, they never quite believed me. From then on, instead of following behind Alekum and me on our walks, they would climb the trees along the road and look down upon us and call out sometimes. There was no more debate however, Alex was definitely a mean dog—or at least it was more fun for them to believe that.

After our stay in Bangui, Alekum followed us to N'djamena, Chad, where he proved incredibly adept at catching lizards and finding cool places to lay in the shade, out of the Sahelian sun.

Last fall, after four years in Africa, Alekum was loaded onto a plane and arrived home with us in Boston 30 hours later. I think he likes life in America, the "land of plenty," where dog biscuits seem to rain from the sky. But deep down, I think he misses Africa. I know he misses the children who used to laugh and follow us around, the goats that were so much fun to chase, and the morsels of spiced grilled meat that we used to bring him from the market. I think the kids miss both of us too, the foreigner that used to talk to them and his strange dog.

Robert Burnham is a programmer who lives for the opportunity to say, "I have a Perl script that can do that!" When he is not fooling around with Linux or wrestling with Alekum in the backyard, he is usually making waffles for his wife, Kathy. They live in Massachusetts where Alekum has discovered New England winters and the joys of snow.

★

The hunting dogs of the Nyanga people of Africa have rights equal with those of the hunters and above those of the women and children. In fact, a hunter will do everything he can to protect his dog from even minor injuries, or discomforts, often at the expense of his own welfare. So, in some ways, he is even treated better than the hunter himself.

Much of this special treatment came about because of the valuable, unconditional friendship dogs offer. Will Rogers once wrote, "That's the one thing the poor country fellow will always have, his pack of dogs, and no man can be condemned for owning a dog. In fact you admire him, 'cause as long as he's got a dog, he's got a friend, and the poorer he gets, the better friend he has."

—John Richard Stephens, *The Dog Lover's Literary Companion*

PAUL   OGDEN

The Roving Ambassador

A grand dame of a signal dog breaks down barriers
to royal treatment.

FROM SEATTLE WE FLEW OUT TO VICTORIA, BRITISH COLUMBIA.
The plane for that flight turned out to be a little twelve-seater, and
though I had been promised bulkhead seats, it turned out that the
seats reserved for us were directly behind the pilot and copilot, I
on one side of the aisle, my wife Anne on the other—and Chelsea,
our signal dog, flat in the middle.
I felt my heart sink as I saw that
the pilot and copilot would have
to step over our dog to get to
their own seats—but they did so
with such obvious enjoyment of
her presence that the considerable anxiety I was feeling about
flying in a tiny plane lifted away.

In Victoria we had a fabulous
time, capped by a special evening
with   my   old   friend   Robie,
whom I'd met at school long, long ago, and his wife Sara. The dinner at the Empress Hotel, where we were staying, was in honor of

> *Signal dogs, often called
> hearing dogs, are trained
> to assist people who are deaf or
> hard of hearing. Along with basic
> training commands such as sit,
> stay, and come, these dogs are
> taught to distinguish three sounds:
> door knocks or bell, alarm clocks,
> and telephones in order to better
> help their humans in everyday life.*
>
> —CH

41

Anne and my ten-year wedding anniversary and my thirty-year friendship with Robie.

We dressed carefully, savoring the feeling of specialness of the evening, and took the elevator down to the restaurant for our six o'clock reservations. The headwaiter greeted us warmly and with a flourish began leading us to our table, but he stopped cold at the sight of Chelsea. I felt time freeze—what was going to happen next? Terribly uneasy, he led us back to the reservation stand and said, "I'm so sorry. I'm afraid the other guests at the restaurant may not appreciate the presence of the dog." We went through our routine and showed the ID card that established Chelsea's status as a signal dog. "One moment," he told us and went to fetch the manager while we held our breath in suspense. Oh, dear, Anne and I said to each other silently. The last thing we wanted was a scene in which somebody might get angry. But an even worse prospect tonight was that our friends' special evening could be ruined, too.

The manager was a suave young man in his twenties. He looked beautifully groomed and sophisticated, but his composure was shaken slightly when he saw Chelsea eagerly wagging her tail and smiling up at him from the plush carpet in the elegantly muted light. I was even aware of a slight expression of distaste as he came toward us with his hand outstretched and a tight, bright smile on his face.

"Would it perhaps be possible to leave your dog in your room for the evening?" he suggested, his smile a mile wide but his eyes almost pleading.

"Oh, no, not at all," I said, with Anne interpreting. "Chelsea can never be left alone in a strange place. But she is highly trained to behave quietly and calmly in restaurants. You and your patrons will never know she is here once we have been seated."

The manager was nodding in a friendly way, but it was obvious that his mind was racing. The suspense built to a higher pitch as he excused himself, still smiling but sweating slightly now. When he returned he had a solution. "I've arranged for a special table to be set aside a bit from the main body of the restaurant so that none of the other patrons could possibly object to the presence of your dog. But there's only one thing—the table will be a bit far away from the band platform, so you might have trouble hearing the music." He caught himself in horror—I could actually see the realization hit that he was talking to four deaf people about listening to the music. For a moment I thought this worldly, sophisticated young man might even cry with embarrassment, but we all rushed to reassure him.

"We haven't come for the music, but for the wonderful food and atmosphere," I told him. "Thank you so much for arranging our special table. I'm sure it will be fine."

Relief turned the manager's strained smile genuine and he turned to the headwaiter and asked him to show us the way.

As soon as we were seated, it was the headwaiter's turn to lose his cool. With everyone comfortably arranged, he looked around suddenly and visibly shouted in panic, "Where is that dog? Where did it go?" In his mind's eye he seemed to be imaging Chelsea sniffing her way through the sea of elegantly clad and nyloned legs, perhaps lifting a leg of her own on a table base or two.

Though I do not know a pansy from a poppy, friends had insisted I see Butchart Gardens about half an hour north of Victoria. Dogs, I was surprised to learn, are welcome at Butchart, so welcome, in fact, that doggie dishes with free flowing water are scattered throughout the spectacular grounds.

—Brian Alexander,
"The Ruff Guide"

"She's here, she's here—under the table." The calm expression resettled itself on the man's face once again.

Three waiters served us during our seven-course meal. The first waiter greeted us warmly and passed out the menus. Then he leaned over confidentially and said, "I hear you have a dog with you? Where is he?"

"It's a she. She's under the table between Paul's feet."

"What's her name?"

"Chelsea."

"I can't see her right now. It's too dark. Would you let the head-waiter know when you are leaving the restaurant? I'd be very pleased to meet Chelsea."

When the second waiter showed up, he said the same thing: "I hear you have a dog with you. I'd love to see her after your meal."

And the third showed the same interest.

Then, as we were enjoying our meal, out came the chef, in his cap and apron, to ask how our dinner was.

"Fantastic!" we replied. "Loved it."

He leaned over confidentially and asked, "May I see your dog?" We promised to send a message to him in the kitchen where we were ready to leave.

After two and a half hours, we were finally ready for a good, long walk. We called the headwaiter and asked him to pass the message along that we were getting ready to leave, and much to our hilarity, not three, not four, but *twelve* staff people came out of the kitchen with the chef. They and the waiters actually formed two rows for us to march through with Chelsea. I couldn't decide whether this was a collection of true and sincere dog lovers or whether the appearance of a dog in that refined atmosphere was too unusual to pass up.

Whatever the explanation, I loved seeing all those people in white beaming at my dog. All of them, remarking on her de-meanor and probably thanking her under their breath for not pud-dling the carpet or frightening a guest, seemed to gather for the sole purpose of celebrating Chelsea's fine nature and impeccable behavior. She walked between them glowing and beaming back, just as she should have done—pleased with their attention but completely, regally, in control. I remembered my initial impression of Chelsea as a fine lady with impeccable breeding. The lady's in her element, I mused, there's no mistaking that. She's probably thinking as she walks down the aisle, "Well, finally!"

Paul Ogden, professor of deaf education at California State University at Fresno, is the co-author of The Silent Garden: Understand the Hearing-Impaired Child *and* Chelsea: The Story of a Signal Dog, *from which this story was excerpted. He lives in central California with his wife, Anne Keegan Ogden, R.N., and Chelsea, their signal dog from Canine Companions for Independence.*

✳

Having public access with an assistance dog has, for me, been a thoroughly liberating experience, although it can sometimes be frustrating, and is often an exercise in patience. The dog, of course, is perfect. The public, however, can be quite another story. Being somewhat new to the more European idea of "well-mannered dogs in the marketplace," American society exhibits everything from a predictable curiosity to an illegal unacceptance. In our three years of public access, Grace and I have experienced it all.

For the most part, people are, at least, polite. One woman very courteously approached me in a grocery store, saying, "Excuse me, but I must ask why you've brought your dog into the store." I told her that Grace is a service dog. She seemed satisfied with that reply, so I didn't elaborate. A few minutes later—possibly after reporting to her employer—she returned. "Excuse me, but you told me that your dog is allowed in the store because she's a service dog." I told her that was correct. "Oh," she looked puzzled. "Is she Army or Navy?" I resisted the temptation to say, "Marines—stay out of her way!" and I explained about her role in my life and the legal provisions made for assistance dogs under the Americans with Disabilities Act.

—Terry Thistlethwaite, "Adventures in Public Access"

GEORGE RATHMELL

In France with Cocotte

An American (poodle) in Paris.

FIFTEEN MONTHS IN FRANCE! IT WAS A MAD PLAN FOR A COUPLE of impecunious school teachers with a sabbatical leave, but we were sure we could do it. And what about Cocotte, our three-year-old poodle? We'd take her along, of course. What's one more poodle in Paris?

We would stay in a hotel in Paris during the week, rent a cheap place for the weekends in the Seine-et-Oise village west of Paris where Margaret had grown up.

We bought a VW Beetle in Germany, and after a few days of sightseeing in Paris, we bought a dog carrier for Cocotte, a bag that encased everything but her head, and took the night train to Frankfurt to get our new car. Cocotte was small, only twelve pounds, so she was easy to carry and proved to be a good traveler. Once back in Paris with our own wheels, we decided to do a quick trip through the Loire Valley, Brittany, and Normandy before summer classes began.

Cocotte was accepted everywhere. No hotel or restaurant ever refused her entry, and most restaurants brought her a bowl of water even before we requested it. She was in heaven. Living on scraps of *poulet rôti*, *bifteck*, and *côtelettes de veau*, gastronomically, she'd never had it so good. Neither had we. We had anticipated that the French would see her as just another of their national dog, but we were wrong. The poodles in France were all the large standard size, and the French had never seen one so small. "*Oh! Elle est mignonne!*" ("She is cute!") was the response she brought everywhere we went, followed by "What kind of dog is it? A poodle? Really? *Oh, elle est vraiment mignonne!*" ("She is really cute!")

When classes began, we settled into a routine. While we were in class at the Sorbonne, Cocotte stayed in the car—we were lucky enough to find parking every day in the shade. We took our lunches in the student restaurant at Lycee Louis Legrand and then had time to walk the dog and move the car to a spot for afternoon shade. We ate simple dinners in the hotel room which meant buying fresh bread every day. We rarely entered a bakery with Cocotte that she didn't come out with the gift of a *sablé* cookie in her mouth.

> *At the Louvre I saw a staircase marked "Escalier du Chien" and asked a French friend if dogs had their own stairs. He said the idea was absurd, but he would investigate. I have not heard.*
>
> —Judith Morgan, "It's Definitely a Dog's Life in France"

Whenever the Sorbonne was closed for vacation, we would fill the front of the VW with our belongings and depart. During our fifteen-month stay we saw most of France, Spain as far south as Valencia, Italy as far south as Naples, Switzerland, Germany, Austria, Belgium, and Luxembourg.

All these voyages took place with no canine mishaps except once. It was in Strasbourg in Alsace. We were in a hotel there, and at five o'clock in the morning, Cocotte let me know that she had to go out—right now! This was unusual, but she communicated her urgency to me, and I, half asleep, threw on some clothes and rushed her to the lobby which was dark and empty. When I pushed the front door, nothing happened. It was locked. Cocotte was frantic. Why didn't I open the damned door? Unable to hold it any longer, she began to poop on the lobby carpet. I scooped her up and ran behind the desk to a back room where I found an unlocked door leading outside. We took a long walk and when we returned, I saw the lights were on in the lobby. I tried the front door and found it unlocked. My first thought was to get some paper and pick up the mess she had made, but I found that someone had beaten me to it. Later that morning when we checked out, we saw a notation at the bottom of our bill, for getting up at 5 a.m. and de-crapping the lobby carpet.

> *While North American restaurants gladly prepare doggie bags, in Europe, where dog food is rather expensive, restaurants frequently wrapped up not only my scraps but almost everything they could find in the kitchen.*
>
> —Carol Baker,
> "Traveling with a Dog"

In Paris our favorite restaurant was La Périgordine on the rue des Ecoles, and we usually ate there when the student restaurant was closed or when we had something to celebrate. It was a small place, but the food was excellent and the prices modest. The chef worked in a minuscule kitchen in the basement, his wife managed the bar and the cash register, and Marie waited on the tables. Cocotte was not only welcome there, she was treated like family. Whenever we entered, Marie would start saving meat scraps for her. The owners had a large German shepherd who lay on the floor next to the cash register patiently watching the activity in the restaurant. There was a large cat there as well who spent most of his time curled up on the bar fast asleep. The first time we went there we were surprised to hear a cooing overhead and noticed that there was a pigeon roosting on the shelf that ran along the walls near the ceiling. When we asked Marie about it, she explained that she had found the pigeon in the street. It had been hit by a car and could not fly very well, so she brought it in to care for it, and it had remained inside ever since. But, we asked, wasn't there a danger of it messing on the customers or, even worse, on their food?

"Oh," she said airily, "that rarely happens."

We kept a wary eye on that pigeon at first until we became accustomed to hearing his voice as an accompaniment to our meal and relaxed. One evening we were too relaxed.

No one had noticed that the cat had left his usual spot on the bar and made his way up to the shelf where the pigeon stayed and was now stealthily advancing on the unsuspecting bird. When he got close enough, he sprang for the kill. The pigeon let out a terrified squawk and fluttered clumsily to the floor, and the cat jumped down after him. It was a warm evening so the restaurant door was open and the pigeon half ran, half flew, out the door and into the rue des Ecoles, the cat in hot pursuit. The German shepherd, sensing that the cat was up to mischief, went after him, and Cocotte pulled her leash free and joined the chase, followed by Marie, then me, then Margaret. It must have been quite a scene to passers-by to see this parade of noisy creatures come pouring out of the restaurant, but the humor was not apparent to us as we chased Cocotte across the street, certain that she would be struck by one of the passing cars.

In due time, Cocotte and the pigeon were rescued, the cat properly disciplined, and everyone was back in the restaurant where Margaret and I finished our dinner with Cocotte's leash securely tied to the table leg.

Toward the end of our stay, Margaret had a lot of conferences to attend in various locations in Paris, and whenever one occurred on a Friday when we had checked out of our hotel, we would have to set up a rendezvous. I remembered a café on the rue de Tournon that the two of us had gone to one day with Cocotte. As we entered the place that day, I felt a sharp pain in my leg and looked down to see a furious orange cat attached to it. The cat had jumped to attack Cocotte and struck my leg instead. Its fur was on end as it yowled and worked its claws out of my flesh and pants leg. A waiter, overflowing with apologies, retrieved the miscreant and tossed it, with a few appropriate epithets, into a tele-

It is customary and stylish in many European cities for an unescorted lady to take her dog along when she goes to a film.

—Robert Scott Milne, "Dogs Don't Lead a Dog's Life in Europe"

phone booth. He told us it was a vicious beast but one that the owner was fond of, so there was nothing he could do.

"The cat's not much trouble ordinarily, but when he sees a dog coming into 'his' café, he goes insane."

We assured the waiter that no serious harm was done, but we sat at our table uneasily because we could see that the cat had not forgotten us. The door to the telephone booth was frosted glass, and the word "TELEPHONE" was spelled out vertically with the letters in clear glass. Thus near the bottom of the door, we could see a pair of yellow eyes glaring out through the lower bar of the final "E." They were fixed on Cocotte, and the hatred and violence that burned in them was nearly audible. We kept Cocotte up on a chair lest some customer open the telephone booth door and release a feline missile.

Remembering all that, I said to Margaret, "I'll meet you on the rue de Tournon at the café with the ornery cat." She agreed and left for her meeting. Naturally, when I went to the café, I left Cocotte in the car. I saw the cat lying on the counter. He looked at me indifferently. Without my dog I was of no interest to him. I ordered an *espresse* and settled down with my book at a table at the rear of the café to wait for Margaret. An hour later she had still not shown up, but with her habit of getting into long conversations, I was not concerned. When I saw her come in, I waved and smiled. She was not smiling.

"What's the matter?" I asked innocently.

"I've been up and down this street half a dozen times, poking through every damn café looking for you," she said angrily. "Just where do you see anything that indicates that this is the Café Henri IV?"

I sat there puzzled for a few seconds and then burst into laughter. "I didn't say 'Café Henri Quatre,' I said the café with the ornery cat!" And I pointed out the telephone booth where the cat had stared murderously at Cocotte on our previous visit. It is not easy to go from anger and frustration to hilarity in an instant, but Margaret did it gracefully with a loud laughing groan that startled the customers and even briefly disturbed the slumber of the ornery orange cat on the counter.

George Rathmell is a native of Berkeley, California, and a University of California graduate who now lives in The Sea Ranch in Sonoma County. His stories and articles have appeared in several magazines and his latest book will be published in 1998. He and his wife now share their lives and travel adventures with Copine ("girl friend"), another miniature poodle who has already been to Greece once and France three times.

✳

We were lucky enough to be given a free course in truffle-hunting techniques by our almost resident expert, Ramon the plasterer.

The supreme truffle detector is the pig, who is born with a fondness for the taste, and whose sense in this case is superior to the dog's. But there is a snag: the pig is not content to wag his tail and point when he has discovered a truffle. He wants to eat it. In fact, he is desperate to eat it. And, as Ramon said, you cannot reason with a pig on the brink of gastronomic ecstasy. He is not easily distracted, nor is he of a size you can fend off with one hand while you rescue the truffle with the other. There he is, as big as a small tractor, rigid with porcine determination and refusing to be budged. Given this fundamental design fault, we weren't surprised when Ramon told us that the lighter and more amenable dog had become increasingly popular.

Unlike pigs, dogs do not instinctively root for truffles; they have to be trained, and Ramon favoured the *saucisson* [a large, dry sausage] method. You take a slice and rub it with a truffle, or dip it in truffle juice, so that the dog begins to associate the smell of truffles with a taste of heaven. Little by little, or by leaps and bounds if the dog is both intelligent and a gourmet, he will come to share your enthusiasm for truffles, and he will be ready for field trials. If your training has been thorough enough, if your dog is temperamentally suited to the work, and if you know where to go, you might find yourself with a *chien truffier* who will point the way to the buried treasure. Then, just as he begins to dig for it, you bribe him away with a slice of treated sausage and uncover what you hope will be a lump of black gold.

—Peter Mayle, *A Year in Provence*

CHARLES KULANDER

The Honorary Huichol

The family dog's work is never done
during a vacation in Mexico.

"YOU'RE GOOFING OFF WHILE I'M OUT THERE WORKING LIKE A dog." We were leaving in less than two hours to visit the most mysterious tribe of Indians on the continent and there they were, watching an *I Love Lucy* rerun.

"Dad," said Olivia, my ten-year-old daughter. "Have you ever seen a dog work?"

She had a point. Boojum, our golden retriever—actually she's more of a dishwater blond—was lying on the bed fast asleep. She was our watchdog, which meant that you could watch this dog do nothing all day long, except occasionally bark at odd phenomena. Like our next-door neighbors.

Do dogs work? I guess it depends on the breed. Each has its own special characteristic. Chihuahuas have a Napoleon complex, German shepherds are into sado-masochism, and wolf hybrids, if given the chance, will eat their owners. Golden retrievers are the Bleeding Hearts of the dog world, overly sensitive, insecure, and wanting to be everybody's best friend. I've seen golden retrievers work as sniffer dogs at international airports. They catch drug smugglers by wagging their tails furiously.

Boojum was our designated guard dog on this trip. I had been training her in defensive attack techniques using my daughter's dolls as assailants. I wasn't sure how she would react to real criminals, but she'd do quite well if we were ever attacked by a renegade band of Cabbage Patch dolls.

Boojum will have her moment, I told myself as we drove down Mexico's Highway 15 on our way to Tepic. Then she will rise to the challenge. The climate turned hot the farther south we drove, and Boojum's only apparent challenge so far was to find a place to soak, such as in the puddles of oil found at most Pemex gas stations.

At a trailer park in Guaymas, a gardener came running into our camp, gesturing towards the swimming pool.

"*No es sanitario,*" he muttered angrily. We ran to the pool, where Boojum was paddling about like the Exxon Valdez, leaving behind her own personal oil slick.

In Mazatlán, Boojum had a chance to redeem herself. After leaving the bank, I noticed the van had a flat. A sports car pulled up alongside, and the driver offered his help. My wife fairly leaped out of the van. In Mexico, she is always looking for a public opportunity to show how a woman can do anything a man can. Jacking up a van was the perfect political act. After the sports car zoomed off, I searched for the cause of the flat. Knife puncture. At the same time, Jil yelled that her purse was missing. The man in the sports car had an accomplice who reached in the front window to grab Jil's purse while she was busy jacking up the car. Dashiel and Livi had been absorbed in their Game Boy. Our only witness was Boojum, who was sitting where the purse had been. This was her moment, I fumed. And what did she do? She did what all golden retrievers are trained to do. She wagged her damn tail.

By the time we reached the Tepic airport, we decided to board her with a local veterinarian while we flew up to visit the Huichol Indians. Big mistake taking a dog on a trip like this, I complained. But the vintage DC-3 that flies up to the sierras was already loading for an early departure. The next flight was in three days. We'd have to take the dog.

"Does she bite?" the pilot asked me, nudging her with his foot. "I wish."

The almost inaccessible mountains of Jalisco and Nayarit appeared disconcertingly close as the overloaded plane droned through the canyons. These craggy peaks have protected the Huichol for centuries, one of the last tribes in Mexico still holding to unadulterated pre-Hispanic beliefs. The passengers were going home for the ceremonies dressed in a psychedelic array of yarn, beads, and feathers, each tassel and design wrought with personal religious symbolism. They didn't pay much attention to us—we came from the same factory as our Levis—but they were curious about Boojum, who lay sprawled out in the aisle, still depressed from her Mazatlán scolding.

The goal was to keep the dogs out of the cockpit. I'd learned that lesson well in 1982, heading for Resolute in the Northwest Territories, when we'd left little gear between the dogs and pilots, and a massive ten-dog brawl had erupted in midair. Three of the hounds ended up in the laps of the pilot and co-pilot, which seemed funny at the time but was in fact life-threatening.

—Will Steger and Jon Bowermaster, *Crossing Antarctica*

The plane bounced hard on the dirt runway, spun around on one engine, and came to a halt in front of a tiny village of adobe huts. We stepped down the gangway and into a crowd of Huichol, who aren't known for greeting strangers but instead stand back with arms crossed, examining you as if you were just another cardboard box coming off the plane. That is, until Boojum bounded down the stairs. They all stepped back in fear and surprise.

A Huichol family allowed us to pitch our dome tent near their *rancho*, in a grove of pine trees scented with wood smoke. After setting up camp, Jil and I left to pay our respects to the head shaman, the high priest of Huichol theology. The Huichol have their own gods and spirits based on a holy trinity of deer, corn, and peyote. The deer is a particularly holy animal. Peyote grows in its footsteps, and visions are transmitted through the antlers, like an antenna to the God Channel. But deer are scarce in Huichol land, almost extinct, and if you could judge by their tiny prongs, antenna reception had been getting progressively weaker.

Before leaving on our trip, Boojum had dragged home an enormous deer antler from a neighbor who had just returned from a successful hunt. After scolding Boojum, we returned the antler, but the next morning—the day we were leaving for Mexico—the antler was back on our porch, while Boojum lurked in the bushes, her head hung low.

"This is destiny," I told Jil, as I packed the antler into the van.

"Look's like petty theft to me," she said.

Jil and I took the huge deer antler to the *caliguey*, a ceremonial structure similar to a Hopi's *kiva*. The shamans were gathered here to celebrate the return of the *peyoteros*, who had just come back from their annual 200-mile pilgrimage to harvest peyote in the San Luis Potosí desert. We were invited inside. Images slowly formed as our eyes adjusted to the orbs of candlelight. Prayer sticks and beaded gourds lay on an altar, along with miniature god chairs and tiny antlers. Men were talking to themselves, lost in a peyote trance, coughing and spitting on the ground. Women pit-patted tortillas while dogs scavenged the ground, fighting over scraps. Presiding over this scene was the head shaman, reclining like Solomon on his throne. We approached quietly, and gave him the antler.

We told him the story of how our dog had brought it home, and that it was our humble offering from the land of Utah. He nodded his approval, and within minutes it was ribboned with prayer sticks and placed alongside the other sacred objects on the altar.

Thinking we had paid the proper respect for admission, the next morning we entered the village with the kids. The celebrations were just beginning. A 19th-century church stood on the far side of the dirt plaza. I walked over and peeked between the locked doors. As I turned, a small angry man dressed in pink pajamas strode furiously towards me, shaking his shaman's stick in my face. In his drunken slur of Huichol and Spanish, the only words I could understand were that he was going to tie me up.

"Hey Mommy, come watch," said Dashiel. "They're going to tie Daddy up."

This was not turning into the Educational Experience I had planned. There are many taboos during festivals—just taking a pencil out to jot down a note is reason enough to land a person in jail—but I hadn't expected to be bound up. The great thing about Mexico is that you can buy your way out of most situations. In this case, the price was a gallon of tequila.

The next morning I entered the village alone. About thirty cows, bulls, and sheep were tethered to stakes in the plaza. One by one, each animal met the same fate, their blood given as sacrifice to the gods in exchange for rain and abundance. With so much death hanging in the air, combined with the cheap alcohol everybody was drinking, it became a little tense hanging out in the village. Some of the Huichol made me a target, throwing prayer sticks at me as if they were darts. Later, one of the executioners held a freshly slaughtered sacrifice up to my face while lecturing me in Huichol. I hadn't a clue what he was saying, but I could imagine: "*You're next.*"

The third day, all of us entered the town, Boojum trotting alongside. Things weren't going as we had planned. There had to be a way to stem this undercurrent of hostility. A group of shamans were gathered around a bonfire, drinking tequila and talking with their followers. The shamans wore round woven hats edged with long turkey feathers that fluttered in the wind. This caught Boojum's attention, as she cocked her head, ears perked. Instinct was kicking in.

"Heel, Boojum," I commanded, just as a tremendous blast of wind hit us. One of the hats gusted off the head of a shaman and hurtled through the air. Boojum paused, tail up, her body lowered into a crouch. Then she bolted.

> *Be sure to tag your dog with name, home address, and phone number. Even more important: make a temporary tag with a way to reach you in Mexico and, on it, offer a substantial but unspecified reward for the return of the dog, if lost.*
>
> —Paula McDonald,
> "South of the Border with Spot"

"Boojum, heel," I screamed. "Heel goddamit," but there was no stopping her. She was running with the wind, chasing after what looked like a Frisbee with feathers. The hat was rolling on its rim when she caught up to it. Boojum grabbed it in one graceful swoop, then trotted back to me swinging the hat back and forth in playful victory while I stood frozen in horror. I took it out of her mouth, hoping that she wasn't about to start playing her second favorite game, tug-of-war.

This is her moment, I thought. Her last moment.

I gave the hat back to the shaman, apologizing profusely for the sacrilege. I recognized him as the one in the *caliguey* when we first arrived. He took the hat without saying a word while looking at Boojum in a curious way.

"Is this the dog that found the antler?" he asked.

I assured him that she was.

"She must be Huichol," he said, breaking out into a laugh. All the others in the group began to laugh as well while Boojum sat on her hindquarters, tail thumping the ground, a lopsided grin on her face. All the tension of the past two days seemed to vanish as they talked of what a beautiful dog she was. No, we couldn't sell her, we said. She was family. The conversation shifted to the ceremonies that would take place that night, which they invited us to attend. After all, Boojum had became an honorary Huichol, and we, her guests.

That night, we huddled in a smoky hut, watching the shamans eat their peyote and sip clear tequila, their dark eyes burning inward. One threw his head back as if in a trance, then began to sing the ancient songs that would last all night long. Boojum lay curled at the entrance oblivious to it all, tired after a day of working like a dog.

Charles Kulander is a freelance writer and travel journalist currently living in Moab, Utah. He never thought of Boojam as a working dog, but now realizes she is laboring in her own mysterious way.

✴

As a puppy our dog Cojin—which means cushion in Spanish, for we had bought him from a street vendor in a Mexican *mercado*—survived a self-induced and near-mortal dose of rat poison. Little by little, he recovered and grew from a round ball of fur into what appeared to be a muscular long-haired dachshund with a pit bull chest. My wife and I adored him, and during a stay in the Italian village of Positano, we had a graphic example of Cojin's attitude towards any other creature who tried to hog the center of the universe—or any other center for that matter. One day as the tourists began to arrive into town, a policeman was stationed in the square where the main road and three or four streets of the town intersected. He was a beautiful sight to see: young, darkly handsome, and dressed in starched whites with gold braid aplenty on his cap and uniform. And he stood with such aplomb, directing what little traffic came through at the time. As he signaled crisply, concentrating on an approaching car, Cojin trotted calmly out into the sunlit square, lifted his leg against the *carbiniere's* white starched pant leg, marked him yellow, and trotted away.

—John Cardwell, "Cojin"

Charley and the Bear

A visit to Yellowstone National Park
brings out the animal in Charley.

I MUST CONFESS TO A LAXNESS IN THE MATTER OF NATIONAL Parks. I haven't visited many of them. Perhaps this is because they enclose the unique, the spectacular, the astounding—the greatest waterfall, the deepest canyon, the highest cliff, the most stupendous works of man or nature. And I would rather see a good Brady photograph than Mount Rushmore. For it is my opinion that we enclose and celebrate the freaks of our nation and of our civilization. Yellowstone National Park is no more representative of America than is Disneyland.

This being my natural attitude, I don't know what made me turn sharply south and cross a state line to take a look at Yellowstone. Perhaps it was a fear of my neighbors. I could hear them say, "You mean you were that near to Yellowstone and didn't go? You must be crazy." Again it might have been the American tendency in travel. One goes, not so much to see but to tell afterward. Whatever my purpose in going to Yellowstone, I'm glad I went because I discovered something about Charley I might never have known.

A pleasant-looking National Park man checked me in and then

he said, "How about that dog? They aren't permitted in except on leash."

"Why?" I asked.

"Because of the bears."

"Sir," I said, "this is a unique dog. He does not live by tooth or fang. He respects the right of cats to be cats although he doesn't admire them. He turns his steps rather than disturb an earnest caterpillar. His greatest fear is that someone will point out a rabbit and suggest that he chase it. This is a dog of peace and tranquility. I suggest that the greatest danger to your bears will be pique at being ignored by Charley."

The young man laughed. "I wasn't so much worried about the bears," he said. "But our bears have developed an intolerance for dogs. One of them might demonstrate his prejudice with a clip on the chin, and then—no dog."

"I'll lock him in the back, sir. I promise you Charley will cause no ripple in the bear world, and as an old bear-looker, neither will I."

"I just have to warn you," he said. "I have no doubt your dog has the best of intentions. On the other hand, our bears have the worst. Don't leave food about. Not only do they steal but they are critical of anyone who tries to reform them. In a word, don't believe their sweet faces or you might get clobbered. And don't let the dog wander. Bears don't argue."

We went on our way into the wonderland of nature gone nuts, and you will have to believe what happened. The only way I can prove it would be to get a bear.

Less than a mile from the entrance I saw a bear beside the road, and it ambled out as though to flag me down. Instantly a change came over Charley. He shrieked with rage. His lips flared, showing wicked teeth that have some trouble with a dog biscuit. He screeched insults at the bear, which hearing, the bear reared up and seemed to

Steinbeck named the vehicle which transported himself and Charley around America "Rocinante" after Don Quixote's horse.

—CH

me to overtop Rocinante. Frantically I rolled the windows shut and, swinging quickly to the left, grazed the animal, then scuttled on while Charley raved and ranted beside me, describing in detail what he would do to that bear if he could get at him. I was never so astonished in my life. To the best of my knowledge Charley had never seen a bear and in his whole history had showed great tolerance for every living thing. Besides all this, Charley is a coward, so deep-seated a coward that he has developed a technique for concealing it. And yet he showed every evidence of wanting to get out and murder a bear that outweighed him a thousand to one. I don't understand it.

A little farther along two bears showed up, and the effect was doubled. Charley became a maniac. He leaped all over me, he cursed and growled, snarled and screamed. l didn't know he had the ability to snarl. Where did he learn it? Bears were in good supply, and the road became a nightmare. For the first time in his life Charley resisted reason, even resisted a cuff on the ear. He became a primitive killer lusting for the blood of his enemy, and up to this moment he had had no enemies. In a bearless stretch, I opened the cab, took Charley by the collar, and locked him in the house. But that did no good. When we passed other bears he leaped on the table and scratched at the windows trying to get out at them. I could hear canned goods crashing as he struggled in his mania. Bears simply brought out the Hyde in my Jekyll-headed dog. What could have caused it? Was it a pre-breed memory of a time when the wolf was in him? I know him well. Once in a while he tries a bluff, but it is a palpable lie. I swear that this was no lie. I am certain that if he were released he would have charged every bear we passed and found victory or death.

It was too nerve-wracking, a shocking spectacle, like seeing an old, calm friend go insane. No amount of natural wonders, of rigid cliffs and belching waters, of smoking springs could even engage my attention while that pandemonium went on. After about the fifth encounter I gave up, turned Rocinante about, and retraced my way. If I had stopped the night and bears had gathered to my cooking, I dare not think what would have happened.

At the gate the park guard checked me out. "You didn't stay long. Where's the dog?"

"Locked up back there. And I owe you an apology. That dog has the heart and soul of a bear-killer and I didn't know it. Heretofore he has been a little tender-hearted toward an under-done steak."

"Yeah!" he said. "That happens sometimes. That's why I warned you. A bear dog would know his chances, but I've seen a Pomeranian go up like a puff of smoke. You know, a well-favored bear can bat a dog like a tennis ball."

I moved fast, back the way I had come, and I was reluctant to camp for fear there might be some unofficial non-government bears about. That night I spent in a pretty auto court near Livingston. I had my dinner in a restaurant, and when I had settled in with a drink and a comfortable chair and my bathed bare feet on a carpet with red roses, I inspected Charley. He was dazed. His eyes held a faraway look and he was totally exhausted, emotionally no doubt. Mostly he reminded me of a man coming out of a long, hard drunk—worn out, depleted, collapsed. He couldn't eat his dinner, he refused the evening walk, and once we were in he collapsed on the floor and went to sleep. In the night I heard him whining and yapping, and when I turned on the lights his feet were making running gestures and his body jerked and his eyes were wide open, but it was only a night bear. I awakened him and gave him some water. This time he went to sleep and didn't stir all night. In the morning he was still tired. I wonder why we think the thoughts and emotions of animals are simple.

Although John Steinbeck made his name as one of this century's finest American novelists with books such as The Grapes of Wrath, *his themes of human dignity and compassion and the virtues of the American Dream extend to all of his work, and* Travels with Charley: In Search of America, *from which this story was excerpted, remains a cherished favorite for many of his readers.*

★

Mutt enjoyed traveling by car, but he was an unquiet passenger. He suffered from the delusion, common to dogs and small boys, that when he was looking out the right-hand side, he was probably missing something far more interesting on the left-hand side. In addition, he could never be quite sure whether he preferred the front seat—and looking forward—or the rumble seat—and looking backward. Mutt started out up front with Mother and Father, while I had the rumble seat; but we had not gone five miles before he and Mother were at odds with one another. They both wanted the outside berth, and whichever one was temporarily denied it would growl and mutter and push, until he or she gained his or her ends.

Before we had been driving for an hour Mother lost her patience and Mutt was exiled to the rumble seat.

Riding in the rumble did strange things to him, and I have a theory that his metabolism was disturbed by the enforced intake of air under pressure from the slip stream, so that he became oxygen drunk. He would grow wild-eyed and, although not normally a drooling dog, he would begin to salivate. Frequently he would stand up with his front feet on the back of Mother's neck, and he would drool on her until, driven to extremes, she would poke him sharply on the chin, whereupon he would mutter, and come back to drool on me.

—Farley Mowat, *The Dog Who Wouldn't Be*

PART TWO

A DOG'S LIFE
AROUND THE WORLD

WENDY SMITH

Wild Trek Dog

Cultures can clash over a dog's role in society.

IT WAS MY THIRD SEASON AS A TREK LEADER IN THE ATLAS
Mountains of Morocco, working alongside the Berber tribespeo-
ple of the region. Accompanying tourists from all over the world
on treks in these high desert mountains, I was solely responsible for
all aspects of the expedition. It was a very demanding job, especially for a woman in an Islamic culture, and could be quite lonely,
among the constant changeover of people.

We were passing through a valley that was rarely frequented by
tourists. The villages clinging to the rugged mountainsides in the
searing heat were extremely poor, the houses made of mud and
woven cedar boughs. Our evening destination was a tented camp
on terraces above the river in a gorge below. On our approach, inevitably, a screaming torrent of children would gush towards us,
plastic shoes flapping, arms flailing, so curious to see "*les Anglais*"
and beg for rich foreign sweets. They were filthy and smelt of animal dung and urine, but were so wonderfully vital and strong, and
quite exceptionally beautiful. The Berbers are originally a
Caucasian race who inhabited these mountains before the Arab invasion following the birth of Islam. They have intermarried and
absorbed the Islamic religion, but still maintain a distinctly differ-

ent cultural identity. Their exclusive gene pool can be seen in the
blue and green eyes and red and blond hair that catches your eye
among the creamy-dark skins. The people are fine-featured and
have an elegance of carriage that defies the back-breaking toil of
their subsistence lifestyle. The children have rosy cheeks over fine
bones, bright white smiles, and a shyness that makes them utterly
enchanting.

In Islamic culture, dogs are unclean. This means they have no
status and should not be touched. The historical provenance of this
notion is understandable. Wild and stray dogs in hot countries
carry disease and parasites dangerous to man. They prey on small
livestock, are generally unkempt and aggressive, feed on human
waste, and have a "sly" or devious nature, the tenacious cunning
essential to their survival. In an environment where man competes
with the elements of both desert and mountain to live, animals are
viewed only in terms of their usefulness. A dog's utility is in providing warning by barking at strangers, or herding goats and sheep.

To Westerners, the treatment of animals in Islam may seem
harsh and barbaric. My experience of living closely with these
ancient tribes-people persuades me that a ruthlessly hard lifestyle
dictates maximum use of all resources, including animals. It was
only 60 years ago that recurrent rape and pillage, massive infant
mortality, hacking at each other with sabers, cutting off limbs as
punishment and piling the heads of enemies at town gates, occurred as normal. When people themselves live in circumstances
we'd wish to rescue animals from, then kindness to animals is a
luxurious concept a poor Muslim can't be expected to understand.

Most Berbers do not hurt their animals purposefully. It is for-
bidden in the Koran. Livestock suffers harsh treatment and is kept
for food or work. But the children, despite angelic faces and bub-
bling laughter, can be unutterably cruel.

My first awareness of Tizi was of a tiny, golden, furry bundle
suspended in mid-air between two ragged boys. A six-week-old
puppy, little floppy ears, slightly paler than her corn-gold puppy
fur, and an almost white baby muzzle with the faintest freckles. She
was squealing a rather angry yowl, and gnawing at the thumb

pinching one foreleg. It was only when her tone changed to a curdling scream that she swung from peripheral vision to the focus of my attention as I realized the boys intended something awful. They were pulling her apart, one foreleg each, back legs kicking her agony into the air. The boys were young, not more than five or six years old, and laughing; enjoying the frenzied reaction they were getting from hurting this pretty creature.

"Hey!" I shouted, furious, striding over and gripping one boy's arm. I rattled off in French, pushing the boys apart. They giggled, enjoying my frenzied reaction even more than the dog's. I grabbed the puppy, who was limp, in what I was to discover was the safest "unresponsive" pose a helpless puppy could assume in the face of such terrible treatment. Children clustered round, all trying to grab the dog. I held her high in one hand and gruffly shouted and pushed them off. Suddenly, this puppy was a valuable commodity. A Westerner had taken an interest. I realized that, now she was a sensation, her fate in the village would be desperate. She would be fought over because I had interfered, and would probably suffer a brutal death.

Deciding what to do was complicated. Because she was a female and would produce more unwanted whelps, she was destined to find an early death anyway, either by torture or starvation. Only male dogs were kept for guarding or herding. Also, I was emotionally involved. I had just returned from Alaska, where I had spent a winter alone, living a wilderness lifestyle with a husky dog team for freighting and transporting. I had come to be totally dependent on the dogs, not just for hauling wood and water, but for companionship, comedy, interest, and a binding friendship. I was very ready for a canine companion, and what better life for a dog than roaming the mule-trails of the high Atlas! I decided simply: she had no future without us.

I knew, within a few seconds of rescuing her, that this was a huge personal responsibility for me, and that her life beyond the summer season was now my burden. I would grow fond of this dog but ultimately have to leave her. However, the immediate circumstances dictated unequivocally that we take her with us, at least out of the village. I kidded myself that we could search for a home for her enroute. I was already smitten by her over-size paws, speckled chocolate eyes, and uncoordinated but enthusiastic energy. So, I arrived at camp with new puppy in tow. She had snuggled into me as I carried her, but remained limp over my arm. It seemed to me that this pup had learned from her short and tough life so far that it was futile to try to defy humankind.

The clients were unaware of any incident when I arrived with this mixture of adorable puppy and parasitic filth. Reactions were mixed. A few were immediately in love, others were disgusted that I could bring fleas so near to their tents. Of course, I could only keep her with their permission. Some were not at all keen. The priorities were to feed her; I was surprised how thin and bony she was beneath the fur, and then to wash her. She was *filthy* and lousy.

The puppy devoured plate after plate of meat and bread. The Berber muleteers were fascinated by my attention to her and concern for her health. Within half an hour the entire group was gathered around this fluffy bundle that was rolling and pouncing, now with enormous engorged stomach, with purr-like growls, and gnawing at everything with pin-like teeth. The puppy had won them over! She was coming with us.

Everyone's first preoccupation was a name. English doggy names abounded, but soon it was unanimous that we choose a Moroccan name. The Berbers were consulted and we had a wonderful evening around the fire, both cultures sharing ideas and language to find a name. Looking at the faces, local and foreign, lit by the firelight as they gesticulated their communications in broken French and Arabic, pigeon-English and Berber, I could see that the puppy had already enriched our lives.

The name we finally settled on was suggested because of our journey that day. We had come through a mountain pass called the "Tizi 'n 'Ourghsan," meaning Pass of the Teeth, and the word "*tizi*" came up regularly on our route, meaning a pass or saddle. All and sundry started chirping "Tizi" into the air and Tizi, obliviously pouncing from shoelace to shoelace, was christened.

In the warmth of the following morning Tizi had her first bath.
You could see the fleas leaping! She hated the experience of being
wet. She stood dripping and
shivering; her resentful glare one
of the first indications of the
strength of her character. I had to
get back to a city to find any veterinary products for her, and
most importantly a flea collar.
After a wash, she turned out to
be the palest gold color, fading to
white at the muzzle. She was
positively adorable, with big rich
brown eyes. Everyone, including
the Berbers, was enamored with
her; she had emerged a happy,
frisky, and inquisitive young dog,
with enormous energy for play
and an immediate recognition of
our social group as her home.

*For anyone who has
ever known the love
of a dog, who has come home and
felt the cares of the day miraculously dissolve before that joyous
welcome of licks, wags, and nuz-
zles, for anyone who loves dogs
and likes to travel, there is nothing
that strips the sweet scales of in-
dulgence from the eyes, nothing
that reminds the traveler how wonderful are the gifts of prosperity
and how great some distances remain, nothing that makes it harder
to sustain a suspension of moral
judgment in foreign lands than to
observe the mindless cruelty with
which poor people in poor nations
so often treat their dogs.*

—Shepard Barbash,
"Canine Culture Gap"

I was surprised by how
quickly she bonded with the trek
group. She instantly understood
the scenario of moving from camp to camp, the boundaries of the
camp, and who was in our party and who was not. She had no previous experience of this, so I assumed it was a natural feature of her
intelligence.

She was just a tiny puppy. Legs at three inches and weighing six
pounds when she joined us, she had the enthusiasm for following
along but was far too small to handle the 15 to 30 kilometers we
walked each day. So, she was packed into the top of my rucksack,
either when she was tiring, or for safety going through a village.
The Berbers thought it hysterically funny that I would carry a dog
on my back. The first day she managed just half a mile. Her eyes
never left me, and her will to follow was obviously strong, but her

weakness was evident; she was soon staggering and panting. With good food she gained strength quickly and grew fast. As she got heavier to carry, she could manage longer distances and became impatient with going in the rucksack. Most of the time it proved a reasonable balance: when she was tired she wouldn't mind the rucksack, when she wasn't, she could walk.

Sometimes we would have to do much longer distances or difficult mountain ascents. On these days it was too difficult for little Tizi to keep up with us and I couldn't carry her because of other equipment I had to carry or other safety aspects of my job. On these longer days I would hand her over to the muleteers and she would ride on the mules. She would arrive in camp strapped into washing bowls, or baskets, or held by a muleteer on his lap. She really detested the mule rides. I assumed it was the lack of freedom; she was generally tied into some restricted space so she couldn't jump off and hurt herself. As we went from trek to trek, she grew bigger and fitter, and by four months old she was lean and muscled and trekking the trails with ease, thankfully without mules.

One might suppose that a wild Moroccan village dog would eat anything. The dog population of Morocco teeters on the brink of starvation and survives by scavenging. As I got to know Tizi I could see how, although she was distinctly a mongrel, she had inherited certain strong traits which equipped her for this hostile environment. She needed almost no water, she managed on little food; she did scavenge, even though she was well fed—and she was mentally designed to cope with such a harsh life.

Psychologically, she was an enigma to me. I had spent many months with Huskies in Alaska, and had studied their psychology and wolf-pack sociology. I saw none of this in Tizi. The huskies had been open and devoted; loyal and keen to please. Tizi was distinctly different, and it seemed to me not just a matter of character but also of genetic provenance. This dog had a wildness of spirit and iron-hard will. She was born to scavenge amongst the rotting waste of the villages and to shy away from humans.

It was fascinating to ponder what wildness and independence was in her ancestry. Cleanliness, and being tied up, were anathema to Tizi. Her closeness to people was due to what she received from them in terms of food and shelter. She had little need for social interaction; growing older she played less and roamed more. Although I adored Tizi, she was not bonding with me. Her strongest feature was a ruthless independence and a stubborn will-fulness to do her own thing.

As manager of the trek I was required to keep impeccable hygiene standards. This meant keeping Tizi clean and under control. Tizi's agenda was the opposite of mine, of course. She wanted to roam free. She couldn't be loose at night and would be kept on a leash at my tent. Sometimes she would curl up with me in my sleeping bag, which I loved; sometimes she would stay outside, and I would feel rejected. One thing was certain: she detested the leash and hated any restriction. Issues of hygiene centered around her mixing with other wild dogs, which she did at every opportunity, and then coming back into camp, possibly carrying parasites or diseases passed from them. She would refuse her food, purchased at great expense in Marrakech, and then be found covered in grime, dragging a sheep's head around at the edge of camp.

It was a big job to keep an eye on her, and as she got older she became wilder and more headstrong. Often I would see a sort of sullen obedience from her rather than happy compliance, as if her innate willfulness dictated some course of action that she knew impossible within the "rules," and the result was a limp dejection and resentful submission. I was troubled that perhaps this was not the best lifestyle for her, but she seemed so much to love the traveling and the people.

The local reaction to Tizi and me was intriguing. It was as if we had become film stars overnight. Village people would gasp and stare as I passed with this golden puppy poking out of my backpack. "*Aini*"—the Berber dialectal word for "dog"—was whispered behind me and, taken up by the children, became a chorus as they skipped alongside.

Soon, we became somewhat famous in the valleys of the High Atlas. I would hear "Tizi!" echo from the hillsides and the villagers would greet us, expectant and curious at this new feature from abroad. In Marrakech I was viewed as terribly eccentric. Suddenly Tizi was valuable; I was offered money for her from rich Moroccans. My trekking crew had overcome their prejudice, it seemed, and would play with Tizi and offer her treats.

It was not until late in the season that I began to suspect that things were not as they outwardly seemed with the Berbers (which I now know is a strong cultural characteristic), and I was to discover just how deeply my non-conformity was disapproved of and how little of that disapproval was shown to my face. I began to suspect that Tizi was not treated well when she was "looked after" by the Muslim staff. Tizi managed to tell me quite plainly herself one day. Sitting beside a well-used mule trail, with Tizi happily sniffing its edges, I noticed the string of our pack mules and muleteers approaching. Tizi stopped to watch them. As they arrived within ear-shot I hailed them, and as soon as Tizi realized who they were her whole body changed. Cowering she hung her head, crept behind my legs, pushing herself into me for my protection. I was deeply moved by her reaction, realizing this was no mere resistance to going on the mules, but a true fear of these men.

Later, I was told by a Berber friend that, although they were sweet to Tizi in front of me, the muleteers would beat and antagonize her while I was away. I was *furious*. But the frustrating truth was that I could only keep Tizi on trek with the Berbers' cooperation, so I made no mention of my knowledge but kept Tizi with me from then on.

As the end of my summer approached, I was desperate to find a new owner for Tizi. Many Moroccans offered to take her, but I could never trust them to care for her beyond my departure. There were no Europeans to turn to. I tried desperately to export Tizi to Britain, my home, or to Europe, but this proved impossible. I was wretched. I had spent almost every moment of this five-month summer with Tizi. I had watched her grow and knew her intimately. Her future was my responsibility and I could not guarantee her safety. And I loved my companion. I spent a week trying to make things work, throwing money at the problem and trying to keep Tizi as my own. But I had made commitments I couldn't be released from, in distant Asia where Tizi couldn't go.

It seemed to me that Tizi's fate had been determined the moment I met her. Her imminent torture and possible death, her helplessness and youth, the harsh culture and hostile environment, my wandering lifestyle and lack of means, all these factors combined to doom her from the start. Although I tried very, very hard, I was as helpless to change things as she was.

In the end I came to the arid conclusion that there was only one way I could be absolutely sure she didn't suffer when I left Morocco. I had given Tizi five very good months. She was healthy, fit, well-fed, happy, and had enjoyed a lifetime that she could not have expected from her beginnings. The only safe insurance that she would not suffer the torture, starvation, and maltreatment normal for her type was to have her painlessly put down by a vet before I left Morocco. I cried, agonized, had nightmares—but found no better solution.

I took Tizi to a charity clinic set up by the EEC in Marrakech for the protection of dogs. The vet there was volunteering his time and, I trusted, was dedicated to caring for dogs. He had given Tizi all her shots in puppyhood. In floods of tears I discussed my decision. He agreed but said that he would try to find her a good home first. I made him promise that he wouldn't give her up to become a guard dog in one of the thousand concrete yards attached to the homes of Marrakech. He persuaded me to leave Tizi with him, and I flew out of Morocco the next day.

I left Marrakech wretched at not knowing what did finally happen to Tizi. I dream of her often, haunted by that uncertainty. I try to soothe my conscience, knowing that I saved her from painful suffering, but I still agonize over whether I did the right thing. I'll never really know.

Wendy Smith is a 35-year-old British woman who has led treks and expeditions on four continents. Born in Glasgow, Scotland, she now lives in Herefordshire, England, but travels extensively. Once a personnel manager

*and army officer, she is now a professional outdoor trainer and expedition
leader. In the Fall of 1997 she began an international expedition, a dog sled
trek across North America. The Website address for this trek is:
http://www.dogtrek97-98.eu.inter.net.*

★

Walking is easy in the Negev desert; the ground is hard solid, despite a
top-layer of scree. In the distance, my eyes make out a gathering of
specks—a herd of goats grazing on a nominal plant life guarded by a
Bedouin shepherd girl who moves with purpose and belonging. I watch
as her herd dogs take off toward the grazers that stray too far. It is the dogs
that keep a herd together, more than the shepherd. I've seen these red-
eyed wolf dogs nudge and growl their charges into compliance, working
on sheer intimidation. I know they are bred to massacre whomever would
dare to threaten or escape the flock.

The girl lets go a curdling yell that riles me more than it does the dogs.
They continue their breakneck run taking no heed of her cries, which
become more and more insistent. It strikes me that the dogs have ex-
ceeded the farthest straying goats and are bounding their lightning speed
toward the only other presence in the desert—me. The lack of authority
in the girl's call strikes me with new gravity as the dogs are now upon me.

The two wolf-jawed and wild-eyed mongrels jump at my feet, grabbing my legs with their paws. I dread my fear the most, remembering that
dogs sense and react to fear severely. I struggle to let go of the terror, but
that makes me focus on it more. I feel claws scratching my legs through
sweatpants, hear them snagging on my sneakers. I try to be still and un-
intimidating and concentrate on calm conciliatory thoughts.
Miraculously, one of the dogs' barking ebbs to a growl and the other one
follows suit. Afraid to move, I remain as I am until the growling lessens
and they begin to retreat.

Now the Bedouin girl is closer, and I am surprised at how young she
is, no more than eight or nine years old. The girl does not acknowledge
me; she turns in the direction of the dogs. I wait for them to retreat a long
way before I take a step, and when I finally do, I step slowly and gently
with an eye in the direction they move toward. Not until I am out of the
desert can I breathe fully or feel adequately safe.

—Naomi Wax, "A Day to Die"

VANDA SENDZIMIR

✦ ✦ ✦

Year of the Dog

A dog lover's journey through China answers her question,
"Where have all the dogs gone?"

ON FEBRUARY 9, 1994, DENG XIAOPING, CHINA'S PARAMOUNT
leader, went on television to celebrate the Lunar New Year and
proclaim the Year of the Dog. Who told the dogs about it? Now
the Year of the Dog is long over, and China does seem to be paying its canines more respect. It's about time.

After three days in Beijing in the fall of 1992, I had not seen a
single dog. In Cambridge, Massachusetts, where I live, I cannot pass
three hours without seeing a score of them: well fed, talked to, petted, as much a member of the family as any biped. The population
of Cambridge is 96,000. The population of Beijing is 9,300,000.
Where were the dogs?

I began to ask, and, as I set off on a tour of ten Chinese cities
and towns, I began to count. As any mother has an ear cocked for
a baby's cry, I, as a dog lover, have one eye at knee-to-ankle level,
alert for fur.

I spotted dog #1 from the taxi taking us to the Beijing airport
for the first leg of our trip. He was a medium-sized yellow mutt
with pointed ears, walking alone and with determination near a
field. I pointed him out to my companion, who said she'd heard
that dogs are banned from the cities.

In the dusty hills above Lanzhou, a large industrial city on the western reaches of the Yellow River, I counted from dog #2 through dog #8. Each was, like her predecessor, a scruffy loner, ambling in a ditch or between houses, nose to the ground. As our tour bus bumped through villages on its way to a Buddhist shrine, I struck up a conversation with a retired businessman from Taiwan. "As far back as the 1930s," he said, "the Communists would come into villages and immediately kill all the dogs, because of their barking. It's become sort of a tradition: no dogs."

The Chinese god Er-lang is provided with dogs as companions as he helps rid the world of evil spirits. It is also a belief that if a dog is running towards you, then riches are heading in the same way. Beware though, if you are dreaming of dogs and get bitten—this apparently indicates that your ancestors are hungry.

—Philip Ramsden, "The Chinese Year of the Dog"

I had already suspected bloodshed. Dogs cannot simply vanish. Where there were dogs, there will be dogs, says Mother Nature. This was the land, after all, of the cherished Pekingese, known in China since the 8th century, darlings of Peking's Imperial Court in the 19th century, when no commoner was allowed to own one. Theft of a Pekingese was punishable by death. This was the land of the fierce and furry Chow Chow, thought to have originated in the 11th century B.C., when Tartar hordes invaded China. This was the land, too, of the recently popular Shar-pei. It was the ancient nursery of the adored Pug. And where were they now? Can the Communists have killed them all?

"Well, of course, people eat them." Many I spoke to, both inside China and elsewhere, told me this. The Chow, especially, has been considered a delicacy. The tradition of eating dogs is strongest in the south. Puppies sit in tiny cages on the sidewalk outside restaurants, next to the tanks of snakes, eels, and frogs, as we display lobsters in the lobbies of seafood restaurants. A standard item on the menu of the Taiwanese army is dog. The Chinese value dogs for their fur as well. Dog-pelt boots from China can even be found for sale in Manhattan.

The picture was growing grim.

I spotted dogs #10 through #15 in and around Xian, China's ancient capital, southwest of Beijing. Dog #10, in a village outside Xian, was a small pooch with short black hair. Dog #11, two miles later, looked like a relative of #10. At this rate, he would have had to be. Dog #13 was an Alsatian, sitting on the bare ground outside a house, watching the traffic and two children playing in front of her. Dog #14, a very dirty white Spitz, was on a leash, walking with his master down an alley

These last two were the first I saw engaged in any kind of doggy work, or doggy-like contact with humans. I started thinking about the places I hadn't seen dogs. They weren't sitting under the open-air restaurant tables, waiting patiently for a scrap from their owners. They weren't walking contentedly with their human families, as these families passed the warm evening hours strolling along their city's crowded sidewalks. They weren't curled up at the feet of the groups of old men who sat on their heels or on tiny stools by the storefronts, smoking and spitting out sunflower seed hulls. They weren't gamboling with children in the small, dusty parks. They weren't, in short, interacting with humans.

I've read that in the past, a past perhaps not yet over, Chinese have been afraid of dogs. They've been bred, almost exclusively, for protection.

For protection of the general population, the government authorities claimed, they had to be gotten rid of. Fear of rabies, fear of attacks. And then there's the waste problem, prodigious enough already, as the Chinese toss litter generously and let their babies defecate in the bushes by any city sidewalk. In America, dog ownership per capita is roughly one to five. If China had even half that rate, one dog for every ten people, there ought to be for its 1.2 billion people, 120 million dogs! Imagine then the sidewalks.

And so, horrifyingly, they have been getting rid of them. Periodic decrees are issued ordering dogs destroyed. In October 1983, the Beijing government proclaimed that dogs have "an adverse effect on social order." Over 200,000 dogs were electrocuted, drowned, or clubbed to death by execution squads. Many were eaten. A fine of $50 was levied against offenders. Dogs could only be kept by foreigners, the police and army, circus troupes, scientific researchers, and restaurants. The American Society for the Prevention of Cruelty to Animals sent a vehement letter of protest; the Chinese government said: Mind your own business.

The Communists have been systematically destroying the dog population since they came to power. After 1949, millions of dogs were executed because they ate food needed for the starving human population. Many were killed to provide fur for the bedding of the Chinese army during the Korean War. But some China watchers think this practice didn't begin with the Communists. Few dogs could have survived the numerous famines that have so relentlessly swept across China. Ross Terrill, author of six books on China, told me that the Communists have just been a bit more thorough than previous regimes, "a function of increased organizational efficiency, of their zeal to tie up any and all loose ends in their quest for control and modernization." While dogs were not one of the infamous "Five Pests," the same thinking that sought to destroy every living rat and sparrow spilled over to dogs.

The callousness of that thinking could only be fueled by the ignoble stature of dogs in the Chinese language. You hear it— "dog" is a common curse word—from the mouths of taxi drivers: "running dog," "dog-temper," "dog-thing," and "stinky dog feces."

Dog days [are] days of great heat. The Romans called the hottest weeks of the summer caniculares dies. *Their theory was that the dog star [Sirius], rising with the sun, added to its heat and that the dog days (about July 3–August 11) bore the combined heat of both.*

—Brewer's Dictionary of Phrase and Fable

But where did the Chinese callousness come from? The dog's close relationship with humankind got its start in the Mesolithic Era as a working partnership—for hunting. In the rich alluvial plain of eastern Asia, Chinese civilization was founded not on hunting but on agriculture. Another agrarian people, the Hebrews, also had no use for dogs and likewise disdained them: dogs who turn up in the

Bible are portrayed as little better than rodents. It was the outsiders of Chinese civilization—the Asiatic herders, the invading Tartars (The Great Khan hunted with packs of 5,000 dogs)—who brought their working dogs with them into the Middle Kingdom. The Chinese assimilated these people, but not their appreciation for dogs.

Dogs are currently banned only from the cities and suburbs. Nonetheless, I spotted dogs #20 through #27 in a city of over 14,000,000 people, in the isolated neighborhoods that cling to the steep hills of Chongqing (formerly Chungking), in eastern Szechuan province. One of these, a tan, erect-eared mutt, was wagging his tail at his human companion—the first evidence I'd seen of canine pleasure. In a field in Fengdu, a town in the Yangtze River Gorges, I saw dog #30 going about his chores, a small creature with tiny ears and very short hair, the exact color of the newly turned earth he was patrolling. He was the closest thing to a Shar-Pei I'd laid eyes on.

In the villages, many families have a dog. And indeed, my ad hoc census multiplied (dogs #31 through #65) along country roads between Yichang and Wuhan, in Hubei province. These dogs generally lolled in front of their small houses and shacks. Bored. The village dogs seemed to be regarded like chickens in the yard, simply there to be fed...and then, perhaps, to feed from.

It occurred to me that the attitude of the Chinese toward dogs is that they are only a slight step up, if up at all, from pigs. We in the West, by contrast, consider dogs only a slight step down from children. To the Chinese, dogs are part of the food chain. To us, they are part of the family. We could no more slaughter and eat them than we could our youngsters. The Chinese could no more buy rhinestone collars and perfumed shampoo for their dogs than they could for swine.

It's not that the Chinese are unused to the concept of animal companionship. Pigeons are very popular pets; on the back porches of many apartments one sees elaborate coops. In Chinese parks old men sit on benches with small bamboo cages containing their pet finches, out for an airing. Even tinier bamboo cages contain pet crickets. But none of these require much food, or space. Food and space are what the Chinese perennially have lacked.

"Look," a friend of mine from Shanghai explained to me, "in America, people's basic needs are satisfied. In China, the majority live on farms. They are very poor. They sleep five, ten people to a room. It's not much better in the cities. The main interest is to feed themselves. There is no space for dogs. There is no extra food for dogs. But things are changing."

Things haven't changed fast enough for the 4,000 dogs beaten to death in Lanzhou two years before I was there. Fifty-six dog-beating squads had gone door to door looking for illegal pets. In Shanghai, another anti-dog campaign was launched in January 1992.

Yet now, on the streets of Shanghai, women wearing the latest styles can be seen walking dogs in the evenings. Dog ownership is gaining popularity, and becoming a mark of status in a land where disposable income once again exists—and can be flaunted. The economic reforms of the past decade have raised the standard of living. There are no famines. Both food and space for dogs are be-coming available.

Space is also becoming available where it matters most: in the heart. The population control policy of one child per couple is contributing significantly to the surge of interest in pets. In the spring of 1993, in the northern city of Shenyang, a dog owner got up the nerve to sue the city for the beating death of his dog by the canine-control squad. "It was not just a dog they beat," said Feng Quantang. "It was a piece of my heart."

So fascinated with dogs are the Chinese becoming that a dog zoo opened three years ago in the countryside north of Beijing. The Divine Land Dog Lovers' Paradise allows visitors, for about ninety cents, to see dogs of numerous breeds in cages and small doghouses. For a few extra yuan, you can have your picture taken with a rare dog, like a Tibetan mastiff, or rent a dog to walk around the grounds. The park attracted 30,000 visitors in its first year of operation. One hopes those 30,000 will be the vanguard of a movement to see dogs for more than their flesh and fur. That is the aim of Xing Lian-jiu, the manager of the park. Says Xing, "People should be allowed to satisfy their desires and be allowed to have dogs. Dogs are the most faithful of animals—even if you have nothing to eat, they will still be by your side."

I caught a quick glimpse of dog #66, my last, on the way to the Shanghai airport. I guessed that there was some Labrador in his family tree, and a bit of terrier. He stood in the courtyard, alone, preoccupied, watching the dense Shanghai traffic. Or perhaps he could see a cat on the other side of the road. If so, he was lucky. In three weeks in China, I saw over sixty dogs—and only four cats. China has no Year of the Cat.

Vanda Sendzimir's work covered a wide range of subjects including social issues and travel. This story first appeared in the North American Review *and won a Lowell Thomas Award for cultural tourism. Sadly, Vanda is no longer around to make our world a better place. She is greatly missed by her husband, photographer David Ludlow, and her dogs, a golden retriever named Bella, and Gracie, a standard poodle.*

✳

Kuiju is reached by a journey of twelve days from Toloman along the course of a river.... There are so many lions here that no one can sleep out of doors at night; for the lions would eat him forthwith.... Though the lions are of great size and ferocity, it is a remarkable fact that in this country there are dogs that have the hardihood to attack them. But there must be two of them.... When a man is riding along a road with a bow and arrows and two huge hounds and chances upon a full-sized lion, the hounds, which are brave and strong, no sooner catch sight of him than they run up to him most courageously, one attacking him in the rear while the other barks in front. The lion rounds upon them, but as fast as he attacks they withdraw so that he cannot touch them, till at last he goes his own way....

—Marco Polo, *The Travels of Marco Polo,* translated by Ronald Latham

LUCILLE BELLUCCI

The Carioca Dobie Derby

Beauty is indeed in the eye of the beholder,
especially at dog shows.

FOURTEEN MONTHS OLD WHEN HE CAME TO US, JEFF WAS TALL FOR a Dobie and an unusual reddish brown, with the standard tan markings. Although his ear flaps had never been surgically made into points, his withers were perfect, his jaw not undershot, his neck erect, though I couldn't tell if it was "dry." The Doberman handbook was written in Portuguese. I didn't expect to understand everything written in it.

We lived in Rio de Janeiro; Jeff had been added to our household after an attempted burglary. He did his job superbly. His roar carried down the block; he nipped any unauthorized hand attempting to unlatch our gate. Once, after first growling in warning, he attacked a voluble guest who seemed to be threatening my husband as he gestured with his hands. Though we scolded Jeff after we hauled him off our guest, we experienced a secret, niggling satisfaction with what he had done. This was the noble dog in action, protecting his master, his hearth, his turf. We had got ourselves a loyal member of the family; blood type was inconsequential. This boy would die for us.

A notice arrived from the Brazilian Kennel Club; there was to be a Doberman show at the Jockey Club. Would we like to enter

Mongol de Leimar? That was our Jeff. His pedigreed name automatically begged for an alias.

And now, to show him at the Jockey Club? I was dubious. I'd taught him about heeling, stopping, and sitting down. What else did he have to do? On the telephone the official said, "Not much else. Bring him in."

The itch for glory was irresistible. We groomed him half to death and brought him in. At the Jockey Club were assembled more dogs than Jeff had seen in his entire life. None, I realized at once, matched Jeff in proportion and beauty. Near us stood an ugly Dobie, with stubby legs and a dull black coat covered with scars. His handler was a tall Brazilian soldier in uniform and white leather gauntlets. I could not keep from staring at them. Compared to my costume, a sundress and sandals, those gloves showed me who the professional was in this business of showing dogs.

The six-month-olds went out. Some heeled, some didn't. Several gamboled around their handlers not heeding any commands. Their antics made me yearn for another puppy. Jeff watched it all; he seemed to be yawning a lot.

Then it was our turn. I had been worried that my Portuguese would not be up to catching the judge's commands, but I needn't have wondered. The orders were abrupt, staccato, composed of single words. Jeff trotted when I did, sat when I stopped. We did collide once or twice. Each time he sat it was on my feet. The dashing soldier's mutt sat neatly and with alacrity, as though his rear were loaded with lead shot.

> *The phobias I meet are very often connected with the show ring. Dogs that won't be handled by judges, men, or women, and who all would be champions according to their owners if only they would stand still for examination—not bite the judge, or stay put on a table, or keep their tails up while being looked at, or sit in the ring.*
>
> —Barbara Woodhouse,
> *No Bad Dogs: The Woodhouse Way*

I caught my husband's glance. He gave me a false smile. We were told to line up in a row: "*Fila!*" Jeff did not want to do it. He had seen his master and was doing his utmost to go to him. I hauled him, my arm held stiff to disguise that fact, into the lineup next to the soldier. As was his habit, Jeff slumped against me. I cocked my knee to push him away, at the same time attempting to stand straight and proud. The judge shot me a look. Perhaps he thought I had a cramp.

An aide carried what seemed to be a bundle of bedding to the judge. When the aide stepped away, the judge's left arm had become three times its original size. He raised his right hand, which held a pistol, advanced menacingly toward the first dog in line, and shot a round past his head.

Jeff's ears flew up. So did mine. He began to tremble, or I did, I'm not sure which. In an uproar of howls and barks and growls, all the outside dogs were straining to get into the ring with us, while Jeff strained to get outside.

"Release!" commanded the judge.

The handler unclipped his dog, who immediately hurled himself at the protected arm and buried his fangs in it. They wrestled together, the judge whipping the dog about the body with the butt of his pistol. He told the handler to retrieve his dog. The handler did so, and then the dog turned and tried to kill him. The judge nodded in a pleased way and moved on. He tested the soldier's dog, who acted faster and more murderously than any of the others.

My placard was doing little hops over my heart. There was nothing for it but to play my ace card: "Rat!" I whispered. "Go get the rat! Go! Go!" It had always galvanized him into action before.

The judge shot his round, Jeff tore from my hand and headed for home. I fled after him. The soldier called after me, "Get a Pekingese!"

At home Jeff reverted to his tough self, but we had learned his secret. His confidence flourished only on his own turf. I suppose there is a moral in here about guts counting for more than mere good looks, that adversity breeds character, and so on and so on. But he was only a dog. I'd just as soon have had him win a blue ribbon for being handsome.

Lucille Bellucci was born in China and at age eighteen moved to Rome. Five years after that she came to the U.S. and stayed for ten years before going to Brazil, where she lived for fifteen years. In her wandering life all the dogs who owned her possessed a sense of humor.

★

Any time I can get to myself to wander around and just enjoy the dogs is special time. I was watching the lakeland [terriers] being judged with enormous pleasure when a mouse suddenly appeared. Who knows whether it dropped from the rafters and somehow survived that terrible fall, or whether it ran out from under the stands, or whether someone with a perverse sense of humor turned it loose? At any rate, there it was, a mouse at a dog show. Spectators, stewards, handlers, and the judge were all taken by surprise, but that was nothing compared to the reaction of the dogs. Forgotten was the endless round of the ring; forgotten, too, were the proddings of the handlers and judges and the hours of grooming that went before. All there was was the mouse and each individual dog, and each individual dog looked as sharp as it possibly could.

Of course, all of the dogs were on leads. One can only imagine with a mixture of mild horror and considerable amusement what would have happened if those born rat-catchers had been loose. All they could do was set themselves up smartly, a whole string of square little red dogs with arched necks, tails pointing toward the dome, noses down and eyes flashing fire. It was like a doggy fire drill. They remained on full alert long after the mouse had vanished. The intruder's progress across the arena floor was not difficult to follow, stringing behind it, as it did, a series of human yelps and squeals, doggy barks and blast, and people popping up out of the folding wooden chairs as if they were spring-laden. The ultimate fate of the Westminster Mouse was never revealed, but he certainly had his moment of glory. He got Best-in-Rodent for that day.

—Roger Caras, *A Celebration of Dogs*

GERRY GOMEZ PEARLBERG

Going to the Dogs

*A celebration of dogs lures a reluctant traveler
halfway around the world.*

UNLIKE 99.99 PERCENT OF THE TOURIST POPULATION, I DID NOT
come to Nepal to trek the Himalayas, but to commune with canines. I planned my trip to coincide with Tihar, one of Nepal's
most important festivals, a five-day holiday honoring Yama, Hindu
god of death, King-of-ghosts, which includes a day-long celebration of dogs.

My friend Matthew, an AIDS prevention specialist at Save The
Children's Kathmandu office, had "casually" mentioned the animal
blessings as part of a not-so-subtle effort to lure me to Nepal.
Knowing my weakness for dogs, he regaled me with vivid descriptions of Tihar, the second day of which honors Yama's pair of
four-eyed dogs, who watch over the path of the dead as their souls
travel through the "barren district" that leads to the City of Yama.
The first day of Tihar celebrates the crow, Yama's "messengers of
death," and the third day honors cows, which, according to one account, are considered "divine rescue boats that take the suffering
soul across the river Vaitarini (mythical river of agony) to
Vaikuntha, the abode of Lord Vishnu in heaven."

The image of a thousand strays wandering the streets of
Kathmandu with garlands of orange flowers around their necks

and red *tika* paste ceremonially smudged on their foreheads was more than enough to draw me. And the idea of spending (at least) one day a year paying homage to man's best friend struck me as infinitely more appealing than the vast majority of Western holidays.

It was not long after Matthew laid his bait that I began actively scheming my adventure. I, who had never crossed the Atlantic—let alone the Pacific—began reading everything I could get my hands on about Nepali culture, about Hinduism and Buddhism, about travel to this unimaginably distant land. My mother kept telling me, "You'll be going halfway around the world," but it wasn't until the trip—which lasted almost twenty-four hours from the time I boarded the Singapore Airlines jet at New York's JFK airport to the moment I set foot in Kathmandu—that I understood, viscerally, the full implications of that phrase.

Determined that my trip should begin on auspicious terms, I chose the day before the dog blessings of Tihar as my date of arrival. As the guidebooks were rather vague about the precise dates of the festival, I contacted Matthew to convey my desire to arrive at the start of Tihar. He called me back a few days later, but there was uncertainty in his voice. The information had been hard to obtain, he told me, partly because the lunar calendar was involved and partly because none of his Nepali friends or colleagues seemed to know precisely when Tihar began and ended. Either that, or they didn't want to let a *badeshi*—a Westerner—in on the secret. In any event, nobody wanted to be pinned down to an exact date, and Matthew warned me that he was almost sure the dates he was giving me were accurate.

By the time my plane touched down at Kathmandu's Tribhuvan International Airport, the combined effects of long hours in the air, lack of sleep, the boisterous throngs swirling about me, and sheer excitement left me physically and emotionally overwhelmed. It was an enormous relief to see Matthew and Laura's familiar faces beaming at me amidst the crowd outside the terminal.

"Hate to tell you, Ger," Matthew said as he started the car, "but you missed the dog blessings. They happened two days ago. I didn't find out till last week—too late for you to change your flights. I'd asked everyone, and they all swore the festival started yesterday, but they were wrong."

My face fell.

"Turns out Tihar began three days ago," explained Laura, "with the blessings of crows; then the dogs, and yesterday the cows."

My face fell some more. I'd managed to miss all the animal blessings.

"But there are still plenty of dogs and cows around with their *tika* powder still on, so after you've had a chance to rest, we'll go check them out."

Acute disappointment was immediately supplanted by awe, an astonishing array of completely unfamiliar sights left no room for dismay. And as luck would have it, while maneuvering through the dusty streets of Kathmandu to my hosts' home in the Bansbari district, we saw many dogs and cows sporting day-old *tika* powder, pink and red, rubbed on their heads. The cows, not surprisingly, appeared to take it all in stride, but the dogs seem a bit startled, some struggling to paw their wreaths of withered marigolds loose, most looking a bit shell-shocked, but happy no doubt for the food offerings they had received, and for the plates of food left out again today for Lakshmi, Hindu goddess of wealth and prosperity. The dogs, crows, and cows had each had their day; now it was Lakshmi's turn. Who was I, a mere mortal—and a Western one at that—to complain? Offerings were scattered everywhere: a coin on a tiny platter of cooked rice, hourglass-like piles of *tika* powders in every

> *Many people will be startled by the way [Saint Christopher, former patron saint of travelers] is pictured in the Eastern Christian Church. He has the head of a dog, but otherwise he resembles the conventional image of a martyr, down to the cross in his hand. The* Menaion, *or* Book of Calendar Feasts, *includes a brief account of each saint's life. We learn from this book that Christopher was a descendant of the Cynocephali, a legendary race of giants with human bodies and canine heads. He is pictured thus in icons.*
>
> —The Monks of New Skete, *How To Be Your Dog's Best Friend: A Training Manual for Dog Owners*

possible sunset hue, raw lentils, apple slices, bright orange marigolds.

"Living in Nepal makes you think of the color orange in new ways," Laura observed as we passed the marigold sea adorning everything from doorways and window sills to the necks of small children playing alongside the road.

I pointed out a large black pup lying fast asleep in the middle of a chaotic traffic circle. A nearby traffic guard seemed utterly unconcerned about the dog and the evident inconvenience it was causing the dense churn of trucks, buses, cars, rickshaws and bicycles trying to pass—they all simply veered around the dog as if it were a fixture or pothole, an immutable aspect of the landscape.

"That dog," Matthew laughed, "is there every day. He shows up in the morning, takes a nice nap right in the midst of all the hubbub, then wanders off who knows where at dusk."

That first night, as I lay in bed too excited to sleep, the otherwise subdued city of Kathmandu was punctuated with the insistent communiqués of barking dogs. The travel books warn of this, and recommend ear-plugs, but coming from New York City where nights are rarely silent, the commotion was more comfort than annoyance. It made me feel secure to be in a city of dogs; a common denominator between Kathmandu and Brooklyn, a bridge between my temporarily suspended life halfway across the world and the vibrant new mo-

So peaceful were they in their daytime slumber, I could hardly believe they would become Hounds of Hell in the dead of night. "They" were the Curs of Kathmandu, and they deranged me nightly with an astounding range of baying, yapping, and howling which penetrated even earplugs and whiskey fog. The torment became too personal; after a while I could have sworn they were barking jamesjamesjames jamesjamesssss.

—James O'Reilly,
"Stairway to Heaven"

ments of my experience here. All over the world dogs speak the same language; a dog's bark is never foreign. Before finally dropping off to sleep, I imagined their howling as a choral tribute to Yama, or as the voices of their shadowy cousins who escort each new day's round-up of departed spirits through the "barren districts" of death.

The next day at sunrise, Matthew and I met up with Dr. Suniti and Sundar, two of Matthew's colleagues, to visit Pashupatinath, Nepal's most sacred Hindu shrine, a veritable cosmopolis of ancient temples, ashrams, sculptures, and inscriptions honoring Lord Shiva in his Pashupati (Lord of the Beasts, or Herdsman) form. The early-morning, pre-tourist scene offers an "authentic" experience, one in which the true beginnings of a Nepali day can be observed: offerings to the gods, blessings, ritual bathing in the river, prayer. And the human worshipers are not alone. Everywhere, packs of dogs and monkeys, co-mingled like relatives, cavort among the sacred sites. The intense proximity of animals and worship to the lives of the people here, the absolute integration of these elements into mundane existence, came as a persistent shock given my culture's unfortunate alienation from both.

Later that morning, we headed to a nearby café owned by an American expatriate, a hippie who traveled to Nepal in the '60s and never looked back. Over eggs and juice, Dr. Suniti regaled us with selections from her abundant store of anecdotes. With minimal prodding, I managed to steer her onto the subject of dogs. This, surely, is the international language; everyone the world over loves to talk about their dog. Back in Madras, she told us, she has a dog named Lassie, whose pups she named Taylor and Burton, and George Bush (Bushy) because, as she explained, "The Gulf War was going on at the time and all throughout India people were naming their sons Saddam, but no one was naming anything after George Bush."

"Sundar has dogs too," Dr. Suniti added, "a pair of very brave and disobedient dachshunds."

This prompted me to mention an event I had recently attended, the Dachshund Friendship Society's annual gathering in Washington Square Park, a memorable gathering in which hundreds of dachshund owners and their dogs converge to socialize, exchange information, and bond over the pleasures and trials of dachshund companionship.

"You Westerners are so eccentric," exclaimed Sundar, before countering with a tale about how his dogs enjoy teetering along the raised ledge of their outdoor terrace—at much risk to life and limb, given that the narrow ledge is situated on the third story level. "Those dogs are so low to the ground," concluded Sundar, "that I believe they relish the chance to get a bit of a view." He explained that this practice of theirs has become something of a local attraction: mothers bring their children out to their terraces for breakfast and distract them by pointing out the "funny dogs" when the kids become fussy or refuse to eat. "No matter how many times I tell those dogs not to get up on that wall," he sighed, "they insist on doing it. They simply crave the view."

After breakfast, I headed off alone, and had an unexpected bit of luck in coming upon a sign-painter specializing in "Be Wear of Dog" signs. In front of his small shop was an array of work; a series of license-plate-sized signs painted on tin, featuring wonderfully realistic depictions of breeds ranging from rottweilers to golden retrievers, set above warning-red lettering in Nepali and English. Thinking they'd make great gifts, I inquired about the price of the signs; they cost about $10(US) each. As I began perusing his extensive collection, inspiration hit: I pulled a photo out of my backpack and showed him a close-up snapshot of my dog, Otto. Could he paint this for me, I inquired. He studied the photograph of my boxer, evidently amused by the huge buttery jowls, the doleful eyes, the goofy expression.

"What kind of dog is this?" he demanded, laughing. Within seconds, it seemed that every man, woman, and child within a two-block radius was gathered around the small snapshot, as if magnetized to the spot by an unseen force. The children pointed and laughed at this obscure creature, and after much peering and giggling, dispersed again into thin air.

"Can you do it?" I asked the man, trying to take the merriment at my dog's expense in stride. He could. We settled on a price and agreed that I would return the following day.

Which I did. When the sign-maker saw me rounding the corner, he waved me into his shop, smiling proudly. He had every reason to beam: his work was beautiful; every detail of the photographic image had been perfectly rendered right down to the rolled leather collar around Otto's throat and the alert yet befuddled expression on his face. Below it, in liquid Nepali script, the bright red warning to "Be Wear." I was delighted, and presented pictures of two other friends and their pups, requesting that the sign-maker do the same thing with these canine images. These dogs, Cooper and Jesse, were a bit more normal-looking by his standards, so this time the transaction was conducted in relative quietude.

The next leg of my journey involved a week-long visit to Royal Chitwan National Park in the *tarai* region to the south of Kathmandu. Just across the Rapti River lies the Chitwan jungle. Gaining passage to the jungle is a strange affair; one pays the boatman a small fee and is ferried a few yards across the deepest part of the river in a dug-out canoe. But the boatman does not take you to the opposite shore. Instead, one disembarks mid-river and wades the rest of the way in waist-high water to the beckoning shore. It is not a hop, skip, and a jump, but several minutes of wading and soaking everything from the belly down. Returning from the jungle, the ritual's reversed; one struggles back to the middle of the river and waits, half submerged and licked by waves, to be ferried the rest of the way. The sight of crowds of villagers standing in the river waiting for their ride, balancing bicycles over their heads to keep them dry, or carrying goats in their arms, was a memorable image that seemed a poignant embodiment of the surrealist state of being we call the human condition.

It was here, on the banks of the Rapti, that I came to know the "gang." Each morning, I'd rise early, ostensibly to observe the abundance of storks, cranes, kingfishers, and other shorebirds that make their home along this quiet river. Sunrise was a peaceful time; the village was still, except for a farmer or two leading his ox-carts across an incandescent mustard field. And the other tourists had not yet risen for their excursions into the Chitwan preserve. For ten days, mornings on the river were mine alone—

mine, the birds', and the gang's, that is. Each dawn, as I crouched in the thick mist along the sandy white river banks, a loosely-knit pack of dogs gathered like a daily convention on the beach.

They seemed to emanate from all directions; a few came loping in from town, some emerged sleepily from the tall reeds along the river's edge, and two or three were always waiting on the beach when I arrived. The sand was pockmarked like a dog paw moonscape; this was their gathering place, and their signatures were all over it. They were a good-looking group of eight or nine dogs, with the curled tails and fine features of basenji's, most about the same size or a bit taller. Their mannerisms were feline, they moved delicately across the sand like panthers, and politely crossed their front paws when at rest. All but two were a deep, buttery yellow; the others were dark brown with yellow muzzles and white stripes down the back of their tails that made them look like skunks when viewed from behind.

While clearly attached to one another (by genes as well as habit), they were an argumentative group; alpha status seemed perpetually up-for-grabs. Their noisy, and occasionally violent, debates over primacy did nothing, however, to interfere with the pursuit of life's finer pleasures: compulsively pissing on each other's mounds of grasses; chasing birds; digging holes; exploring the flotsam and jetsam upon the beach; scavenging; snoozing in the sun; splashing in the river; snapping at flies; and playfully antagonizing one another in a thousand and one creative ways.

Day after day, I came to photograph them, the dogs of morning mist, and day after day their personalities emerged. There was "Elsa," the largest and most golden-colored of the group, a sleek girl who, in alert repose, resembled nothing so much as a lioness. She spent a lot of time watching me, and let me get as close as I liked to take her sphinx-like portrait in the sand. There were the "Gemini Twins," the playful youngsters of the group, who constantly entertained themselves by gnawing on each other's paws. And "Zipper," a black dog bearing a long pink scar along his flank, who came each morning to the beach, not to socialize, but to dig deep holes in the sand, into which he then settled, and assiduously guarded.

"Scarface" was another member of the pack who seemed to have a nose for trouble; anytime an altercation broke out, she was dead smack in the middle of it. And then there was "Phantom," one of two very light-colored, almost translucent dogs who never seemed to emerge from anyplace in particular; not from the tall grass or the road leading to town or the little farmhouse down the river, but manifested as if borne of the fog itself.

The Gemini Twins had a knack for finding toys on the beach. On my first morning, they discovered a pink rag to play with, each pup pulling at an opposite end in a colorful tug-of-war that attracted the other dogs. Within minutes, teams were drawn up, and a chaotic game of rip-the-rag ensued, resulting in a frenzied pile of yapping, kicking, and canine competition. At some point, the rag was rent in too many pieces to make group play worthwhile; the inseparable twins wandered off together to chew on a couple of tiny remnants, and the others ambled down the beach together, presumably in search of breakfast. They hadn't gotten far when one of them let out a bone-wracking howl—more a screech than a call—having apparently found something worth writing home about. That's when the fight broke out over the fish carcass, and I headed back into town to buy some breakfast of my own, and a dozen extra yak cheese sandwiches to share with the obviously ravenous gang.

For each of the nine mornings that followed I shared yak cheese sandwiches with the dogs of Sauruha. I was sad to say goodbye.

The return from Chitwan to Kathmandu marked the end of my trip. On my final day, as my airplane taxied down the runway, Nepal presented me with a final omen: a small dog appeared alongside the edge of the runway, trotted alongside us for a moment or two, then stood stock-still, fixedly watching with the stern and loving concentration of one of Yama's own, as we rose into the atmosphere and irrevocably away.

Gerry Gomez Pearlberg is the editor of Queer Dog: Homo/Pup/Poetry *(Cleis, 1997). Her book of poems,* Marianne Faithfull's Cigarette, *is forthcoming from Cleis in 1998. She lives in Brooklyn with her boxer, Otto.*

✳

In Tibet, where wolves and brigands prosper, the nomads' camps and remote villages are guarded by big black or brindle mastiffs. Such dogs are also found in northern Nepal, and last year in the Bhote Khosi region GS [the author's companion] was set upon by two of them that were guarding some Bhote packs left on the trail; he narrowly escaped serious injury. The mastiffs are so fierce that Tibetan travelers carry a charm portraying a savage dog fettered in chain: the chain is clasped by the mystical "thunderbolt," or *dorje,* and an inscription reads, "The mouth of the blue dog is bound beforehand." During the day the dogs are chained; at night they roam as sentinels and guards. In the first of the Dhorpatan encampments, we walked the center of the mud thoroughfares to avoid the snarling, straining animals on both sides. Then one of these broke or slipped its chain and came for us from behind, without a bark.

Since GS was several yards ahead, I was selected for attack, which was thwarted only in the last split second. Luckily, I heard it coming, and swung around upon it with my heavy stick: the beast tumbled back and then came on again, snarling now in a low, ugly way. Searching in vain for a heavy rock, I did my best to crack its skull, while the dog lunged back and forth at the tip of my stick in horrid fury. Meanwhile, GS had located a heavy split of wood; he hurled it at the dog with all his force. The brute dodged, then sprang after it, sinking its teeth deep into the wood. Finally, it was driven off by a Tibetan, who until now had watched calmly from the doorway of his hut to see how I might fare. From Dhorpatan north across the Himalaya, it was said, such dogs were common, and I never walked without my stave again. If I had not cut it in the hour before (after eight days of getting by without one), I might have been hurt badly, and I marvel to this day at the precise timing.

—Peter Matthiessen, *The Snow Leopard*

MICHELE LEVY BENDER

They Don't Take
Just Any Mutt

And you thought getting your child into
a good preschool was hard.

PARKS COMMISSIONER HENRY J. STERN'S SOLUTION TO THE PER-
ennial problem of leashless dogs in Central Park is the neighborhood dog run. Evidently, he has never tried to join one. In New
York, it takes an endless wait and a sizable check to set your dogs
free.

For years on our 6 a.m. walk, my husband, David, and I wrestled with our golden retrievers, Willi and Dune, as they feasted on
the gourmet garbage from our SoHo neighborhood: seared tuna
from Zoë, Thai noodles from Penang, and focaccia from Dean &
DeLuca. Tired of this tug-of-war, we decided to sign up for the
Mercer-Houston Dog Run, a fenced slab of concrete adjacent to
New York University that contains a plastic swimming pool and
four park benches. Willi and Dune would retrieve tennis balls
while we peacefully sipped coffee and read the paper. No more
morning battle of wills, no more snacking on trash.

"I'll put you on the waiting list," said a woman who answered
the phone at the dog run. Waiting list? Had I reached N.Y.U. ad-
missions by mistake? "I'm just the service, ma'am," she said and
hung up. Weeks passed without word. I called back, describing
Willi and Dune, vainly hoping she would be swayed by their

charms. Instead, she grew annoyed. When we walked by the run
Willi and Dune barked at the dogs inside. "You're just as good as
they are," I said consolingly.

Six months later, I came home to a message that an application
was in the mail. I shook the dogs awake.

"You're in, you made it," I cried, too caught up to realize that
they hadn't dwelled on this for months. Later, I realized the message didn't say we had been accepted. I had heard ridiculous stories about waiting lists and interviews for kindergarten, but a dog
run? Would there be an essay? "Relax," David said. "If it's that elit-
ist, we don't want in." But I felt differently. I wanted that key. I
wanted our dogs to belong.

I carefully filled out the form. One question that stumped me
was: "Please describe any special talents you can donate to the
run." My homemade carrot cake? I left it blank. Another month of
silence. Finally, a phone call: "Bring your entire family and both
dogs," a dog run member commanded.

Orientation morning, I brushed Willi and Dune until their
coats glistened like honey. I prayed Willi wouldn't do that thing
where he drags Dune on his back across the floor with a rope.
What if they didn't pay attention when we said "sit" and
"rollover?" Golden retrievers are known to be dumb.

Sam, a tall, thin man in a suit, met us outside the run. He ran
his fingers through his white hair and then swung open the gate,
stepping out of the way like a bellboy at a fancy hotel. His fluffy
bichon frise, Question, sat quietly at his feet.

Sam began to recite pages of rules detailing potential behavior
problems. By the end, I half expected him to hand me a list of canine shrinks. When he finished, he mentioned the $90 fee for
membership. Finally, he opened his large hand, slowly revealing a
gold key. He paused a moment. "Welcome to the run," he said in
a soft serious voice. At last I held the key. But inside I felt empty.

Our mornings began to change. On the way to the run, Willi
and Dune now ate garbage from the previous night's gallery open-
ings. We had another key to remember. And tennis balls to carry.
When Willi and Dune swam in the pool, our apartment smelled of

wet dog for two days, and black paw prints covered our floors. Most of the dog-run members ignored one another.

"It wasn't like I thought it would be," I told David after a few weeks. Soon the four of us were back to the old route, to the Dean & DeLuca crusts.

On the rare occasions when we still visit the run, I see dogs and their owners looking longingly at us from outside the gate. To them, dog-run life looks glamorous and exclusive. If they only knew.

Michele Levy Bender has lived in SoHo for the past six years. This story originally appeared in The New York Times.

★

Growing up in suburban Baltimore was simple: kids went to school, adults went to work, and dogs ran around in backyards. Imagine my surprise when, as a prospective graduate student visiting the Big Apple, I was introduced to the Urban Dog. I did see some dogs on leashes. But I also saw dogs in bicycle baskets, in shopping carts, on leashes—pulled by owners on Rollerblades, or next to owners on bicycles. Some dogs were even being carried in gym bags (zipper slightly open, of course!), in Snuglis (baby carriers), or in baby strollers.

In fact, the New York City Parks Commissioner, Henry Stern, a self-described "man for all species," is a dog lover and dog owner himself. His golden retriever, Boomer, (always on a leash!) accompanies him to meetings and appearances throughout the five boroughs. Mr. Stern even keeps a counter in his pocket at all times, hoping that friendly New Yorkers will put him and Boomer in the *Guinness Book of World Records* as the "Most Petted Dog in the World."

—Howard Blas, "Dogs in the Big Apple"

Tourist Dog

An American couple living in Bali
provide their hosts with a new
way to view dogs.

THE BALINESE BELIEVE THAT DOGS ARE THE REINCARNATED SOULS of Javanese thieves. To appreciate this notion fully, you should know that in Bali, thieves caught in the act are liable to be mobbed and beaten, even killed, and that the Balinese believe most evil-doing generally originates in Java.

A Balinese dog spends his short, miserable life slinking along the lanes, tail between bowed legs, nosing for garbage scraps and creepy-crawlies. When tired of kicking him around, his masters may well turn him into dinner. Only the approach of unarmed strangers gives him a precious shot at self-respect, and he will make the most of it: barking, growling, and feigning attack. Should he actually attack, however, his owner will kill him immediately. (If you don't trust in the power of natural selection, carry a stout walking stick in Bali.)

When my husband, Jerry, and I first settled down to live and write at Sari Bamboo, in a two-story house overlooking an emerald sweep of rice fields, our landlord's two dogs formed an unwelcoming committee whenever we came home. Within a few days, the fierce barking simmered to low growls. By the end of the first week, they didn't lift their heads. Still, nothing about the two in-vited overtures of friendship.

The older dog, Opah, gave plausibility to the reincarnated thief theory. A wolfish brute with shifty eyes, he led a gang of tough mutts who fed on table scraps from tourist restaurants. We often met him far from home, roughing up some smaller dog. Djarum, named after a popular brand of cigarettes, had a more mellow temperament. He was skinny, homely, and half wild. Still, some-thing about him appealed to us: maybe the protruding canine teeth that pushed his mouth into a silly grin, or his compelling yellow eyes.

The Indonesian islands are inhabited by 300 ethnic groups with distinct cultures, speaking 365 languages and dialects. Despite the national motto "unity in diversity," these cultures are under threat from Indonesianisa-tion as the islands are gradually unified under centralized Javanese rule.

—CH

One night not long after our arrival, we were awakened by shouting and swearing, accom-panied by thudding feet. A bold thief had broken into the house next door, creeping halfway to the second floor before the American tenant chased him downstairs and outside. The thief—universally described as Javanese, although no one ever saw him long enough to prove this—escaped into the rice fields with a bagful of expensive items. This outrage prompted an onslaught of security measures by our landlord, Wayan Sari, who augmented the shuttered windows with bamboo bars and added his ancient father to the family staff as guard. This smiling little man, serene and gentle as a monk, fulfilled his new function by sleeping on the family porch—a considerable distance from ours.

It wasn't long afterwards that I caught Jerry sidling up to Djarum with a handful of *krupuks*, the Indonesian snacks that look like styrofoam and taste like shrimp-flavored air.

I watched the surprised dog snatch the *krupuks* and shrink back with a warning growl. "What are you up to? These guys aren't pets, you know; they're watch dogs."

"Exactly. More where that came from," Jerry told the dog, who raised his head to watch us walk down the path to our bungalow.

After dinner that evening, we stopped to greet Wayan Sari; his wife, Wayan Martini; and their baby son, Wayan Endra. (For obvious reasons, we referred to them as "the Wayans." This was not a family name—these don't exist in Indonesia—but a birth order name, "First Born," that they happened to share.) During the pleasantries and small talk that are an essential element of Balinese life, I noticed Djarum inching ever so subtly toward us, his great yellow eyes fixed on Jerry's day pack.

When we arrived at our own porch, I heard panting behind me. There, below the porch, hovered Djarum, gazing anxiously at the pack Jerry was laying on the glass top of the bamboo coffee table. The metallic screech of the zipper sent his tail switching like a metronome. Jerry smiled and slowly pulled out a waxed paper bundle oozing meaty juices. Djarum, whining low in his throat, was tempted into placing his paws on the lowest step.

Jerry offered him the bundle. "Like chicken *satay?*"

Djarum could resist no longer. In one frenzied leap, he landed on the porch and inhaled the meal, undoubtedly the finest of his life. Then, sitting back on his haunches, he gazed adoringly at his benefactor.

"Good dog." My husband reached a tentative hand toward the dog's head. "*Anjing bagus!*"

I held my breath, expecting a mighty snap. Twisting around to meet the hand, Djarum growled, then sniffed the hand that had just fed him. But when Jerry tried to pat his head, he snarled and bolted.

A week later, I sat in one of the big bamboo porch chairs—my office—typing away on my laptop computer. Jerry was cursing at our rented Indonesian PC clone, the bane of his existence. An exquisite scene lay before me, framed by hibiscus and frangipani bushes. Against a backdrop of coconut palms, their fronds shining like glass, terraces of deep green rice were punctuated by stone shrines and the grass-roofed huts which sheltered farmers from the mid-day sun. The balmy air was busy with the contented quack-

ing of ducks, the shimmering of a distant gamelan, and—less
lyrically—the annoying whine of motorbikes on the Penestanan
Road.

It was hard to work with all these pleasant distractions, so I was
happily relieved when Wayan Martini, fresh and lovely in a loose
dress of blue and white batik, arrived to visit. Hovering on our
steps, she greeted me with one of her radiant smiles.

"Busy, Meri?"

Our busyness was a constant source of awe. "Foreigners work
very hard," Wayan would marvel as she watched us working right
up until sunset. She worked hard, too, but with plenty of time off
for socializing and the frequent celebrations that color Balinese
life.

"Only a little busy, Wayan." Saving my file, I clicked off the
computer. "Please!"

Leaving her flip-flops on the lowest step, she took her customary seat on the edge of a chair. Balinese people, though friendly to
foreigners, tend to think the rest of the world does not compare
favorably to Bali. Wayan may have privately agreed, but her deep
and never-ending curiosity about the greater world led her to improve her English, read foreign books, and ply her guests with
thoughtful questions. Today, undoubtedly, there was some puzzling
aspect of Western culture she wished to clarify, but before she
could open her mouth, a look of horror froze her pretty face.

Following her gaze to the sofa, I saw through her eyes. On the
batik-covered sofa cushion, once bright but now dimmed with
dog dirt and hair oil, snoozed Djarum like a pampered lap dog. He
didn't look like one of those, however. His ear was torn and bleeding—a warning from Opah, perhaps, to stop kissing up to
tourists—and even in sleep one leg gently kicked at fleas. His balls,
impressive in their size and bareness, were prominently displayed.
And it's true that while you can lead a dog to water, you can't necessarily make him bathe. Djarum's stench was awesome.

As Wayan caught her breath, I stammered excuses: "Jerry's
idea...security...thieves—Javanese, of course..."

Djarum, sensing trouble even in his dreams, had awakened and scrambled to the floor. As he slunk past his owner, her bare foot shot out and kicked him to his rightful place: the outer limits of the porch.

"Meri." She gulped. I could see her hunting desperately for some way to excuse our behavior. "Maybe in America…?"

But she could not go on.

Wayan Sari's young sister Nyoman, resplendent in full temple regalia, saved the day by appearing with the household offerings: flowers, rice, and smoking incense on trays fashioned from banana leaves. (Since receiving the protection of daily offerings, the computers had been functioning much better—although Nyoman was a bit surprised when we asked her not to sprinkle them with holy water.) Giving her sister-in-law a quizzical glance, she slipped inside our house.

During the interval, I had seen a way to get off the hook. "In America, dogs often sleep on sofas, Wayan, but usually they have their own special pillows."

"Dogs…having pillows?" Wayan closed her eyes, trying to imagine this.

"In little beds. Covers, too."

She raised a delicate hand to her forehead. "Covers," she repeated faintly, probably thinking of the heavy—and expensive—*ikat* cloths that covered her guest beds.

"Oh, dogs have all kinds of special things. Toys…" I was really getting into this. Compared to the excesses of American society, what was a dirty sofa cushion or two here in Bali? "Wayan, in America people love their dogs so much that they give them leather collars, with jewelry sometimes, and in cold weather, they dress them in little sweaters."

Wayan frowned at a giant wasp sailing between us. I knew she was listening; she simply couldn't muster a response.

"There are workers who only give dogs baths and manicures and haircuts," I continued. "That's all they do. Some people have the job of taking dogs for walks, or teaching them to obey orders and do tricks, or taking care of them when the owners go on vacation."

"*Pembantu* (helper) for dog?" Wayan whispered.

I ducked as a tokay dropping, looking just like a Greek olive, plummeted past my nose. The big lizards stayed out of sight, but they made their presence known with heart-stopping croaks and well-aimed missives.

"Yes, Wayan, many jobs for taking care of dogs," I said, lapsing into Bali-speak. "Even giving dogs massage."

"Dog massage? Good job for tourist. Maybe can giving for Bali dog at Kuta Beach," joked Wayan. With her usual resilience, she was already leaving the realm of the unthinkable. "But Meri, I am thinking maybe, only rich people do like that?"

Should I blame everything on the idle rich, whose excesses were already familiar to her via five-star tourism? Or admit the truth?

I opted for the truth. "Wayan, in America most people do like this. The supermarket has special foods for dogs, expensive food," I added, brightening as I saw a whole new avenue of surprises opening for her. "And Wayan—they actually raise cows for dogs to eat."

Even before I saw her eyes widen, I regretted saying that. Along with Hinduism, the notion of sacred cows had traveled here from India. But instead of letting their cattle wander, free to starve unmolested, the pragmatic Balinese sell them to the Muslims in Java.

I tried to give her a broader perspective. "Wayan, in America, people don't think dogs have evil natures."

She turned to look at Djarum, who happened to be demonstrating his demonic origin by devouring the offerings Nyoman had left on the ground for the *bhutas* and *kalas*, the earth spirits who torment human beings if not so placated.

"America people very strange," Wayan ventured, with a shy glance to make sure that I was not offended.

"Yes, they can be." Abandoning the idea of explaining dog shows, I thought of something closer to her experience. "When dogs die, some people have funerals for them! Like cremation," I added, seeing her confusion.

But this was a mistake. In Bali a cremation is a grand event, terribly expensive. It is also an essential religious duty of the family. Until enough money is raised for a cremation, which can take years, the soul must wait, trapped within a rotting body, for its passage to another form or—ideally—union with God.

All this for a dog? I could see Wayan struggling between the humor and the blasphemy of the notion. Then her forehead wrinkled as another unpleasant thought occurred to her.

"Meri, in America dog not coming in house...?"

I remembered how Djarum would stand at the open door looking wistfully in at Jerry, but never, ever set one paw inside. "Well, yes, sometimes they do. Some dogs have their own houses."

There may be no worse fate than to be reincarnated as a dog in Bali. The mangy curs are abused by day and cursed by night, for when darkness falls they raise their voices in howls of indignation as though warning their human masters that this fate could be theirs should they fail to lead a moral life. But for all the abuse heaped on these dogs, the Balinese can be remarkably sensitive when foreigners lose their beloved pets. Often they will wrap the animals in shrouds, scatter flower petals upon them, and perform a funeral rite to ease the loss.

—Larry Habegger, "Bali Dreams"

"Meri!" Clearly, Wayan was beginning to wonder if she could really trust the source. "House for dog?"

"Very little houses," I assured her. "And if a husband makes his wife angry, she won't speak to him. Then people say, 'He's in the dog house.'"

Comparing a man to a dog! This was too great a dose of cross-cultural revelation to swallow in one sitting. Gathering her skirts, Wayan rose gracefully. "Thank you, Meri, for telling all these interesting things. I must think about this."

After that, Djarum made sure his cozy relationship with us was never witnessed by the family. The sound of footsteps coming up the walk was the signal for him to fly off his (by now disgusting) sofa cushion. However, the Wayans couldn't help noticing how he had deserted them.

One night as we passed the family porch, Djarum fell into place as usual behind us. I heard a burst of laughter and a scornful, "*Anjing touris!*"

Tourist dog. I had a sudden, dreadful thought. What would happen to Djarum when we left Bali? Already he was following us down to the local restaurants. He would enter confidently, only to be booted out—not, unfortunately, before causing us extreme embarrassment. He had acquired foreign tastes in food and in his expectations of what a dog's life should be. He loved being petted and scratched behind the ears, and had developed puppyish ways such as racing around and around the garden when excited by too much play.

And what about Jerry? He had grown fond of Djarum, absurdly fond. He even had a collection of doggy photos now. What if we came back to Bali one day, only to discover that "our" dog had been turned into *satay anjing*?

I wish I could report that Djarum finally won glory or at least respect in Wayan's eyes by foiling a second burglary attempt. What a fine story that would be, nicely rounded, and a vindication of our foreign ways. For all we know, he did scare away a thief or two, without any way to tell us of his exploits. All we knew for sure was that one day when our friend Lyly stopped by to leave us an important message, he refused to let her near our porch.

A month after leaving the island, we heard from a friend that "our dog" was often spotted moping around our former haunts. Wrote Max, "His face still has this expression: Abandoned, abandoned!!"

The image saddens me, but not as much as it would if I didn't suspect that at this very moment, Djarum—the apple of some tourist's eye—is snoozing blissfully on a by now unspeakable batik cushion, his heart warm and his stomach full of chicken *satay*.

Meredith Moraine spent eight blissful months in Bali writing a murder mystery novel with her husband, Jerry Steward. The Kris of Death, published in Indonesia, is the first of a series featuring globe-trotting writers much like themselves. "Tourist Dog" is taken from a work in progress about Meredith's cross-cultural misadventures with their delightful landlady and other Balinese friends.

✳

Every evening at sunset, the dogs would slink out of bamboo thickets and overgrown jungle caves, the black earth still clinging to their muzzles, and invade the tiny village of Ubud. They would gather at the foot of the hill where I was staying, two kilometers north of the village, and organize into packs. I could hear them from my rented hilltop bungalow, howling as they spread out over the one road through the center of Bali and moved south to the village where they would roam the deserted paths all night, occasionally pausing to scavenge for food, battle, mate, or regroup. Though everyone, villagers and travelers alike, hated them, there seemed to be no easy way of stopping the dogs.

—Faith Adiele, "The Transmigration of Souls"

THOMAS LONG

Dog Soldier

A journalist meets the softer side
of a Central American hit man.

HIS NICKNAME WAS MICO (MONKEY), AND HE WAS SAID TO BREED dogs, among other things.

We were mostly interested in the other things.

It was 1990. The Berlin Wall had fallen, but some of the Cold War's fiercest adjunct players in Central America were still engaged. It seemed a good time to finally interview the infamous Mario Sandoval Alarcon.

El Mico was known in some circles as the godfather of Central America's death squads. He rose to prominence with the 1954 coup engineered by the CIA that overthrew Guatemala's democratically-elected leftist government of Jacobo Arbenz. The motive was to stop the spread of Communism in America's backyard, and to ensure the continued freedom of the United Fruit Company to maintain its banana empire without interference.

For much of the 35 years following the coup, the military ruled Guatemala in an iron-fisted reign of terror with the political support of Sandoval's Movimiento de Liberacion Nacional (MLN). An estimated 100,000 Indian peasants, leftists, and labor organizers were killed or "disappeared" in the ensuing decades.

And always, the figure of Sandoval loomed large.

In her book on Guatemala of the 1980s, journalist Jean Marie Simon had told of her own earlier encounter with Sandoval. Sitting in his car waiting for him while he went off to meet someone, Simon wrote, the bodyguard/driver turned to her and explained that he normally charged about $50 to kill someone. But since she was a friend of his boss, he would perform a job for her for free, if she ever needed it.

With this as background, my wry cohort Colum Lynch and I were sent to interview the godfather by our boss at *The New York Times*, who himself had dubbed Mico "the Darth Vader of Central America."

The reference was partly due to the ominous reputation of the man who had proudly claimed that he had fashioned his political movement after Generalissimo Francisco Franco's Falangistas. The other reason was that Sandoval had a tracheotomy for throat cancer, which left him with a mechanical voicebox in his throat through which he communicated via a series of fetid belches that one had to listen very closely to understand.

We had been covering the civil wars in Nicaragua, El Salvador, and Guatemala. We had seen far more grisly death than many people will in a lifetime. I had witnessed up close the handiwork of the infamous White Hand, the Secret Anti-Communist Army, and others. But a visit to the inner sanctum of Mico Sandoval would be a new experience indeed, fraught with all the myth and legend of the man who was once quoted as calling his movement "the party of organized violence."

Liberation Boulevard is a long stately thoroughfare that forms a strategic border between Guatemala City's wealthy district and the air force base. It is a commercial avenue, populated by car lots, restaurants, and other businesses. There is only one residence on the entire boulevard, and that is Sandoval's. It was named after the coup—which he called "The Liberation"—and no matter what else occurred along that street he was damn well going to have that as his address.

We pulled into the drive in the morning, greeted by the uneasy presence of a half-dozen large bodyguards with dark eyes and darker souls brandishing Uzis, shotguns, and automatic pistols. They frisked us with a professional humorless efficiency, and then an electronic buzzer opened the heavy iron door.

The foyer entrance was a grand atrium dominated by the largest portrait I had ever seen. It was a painting about eight-feet high of Colonel Castillo Armas, a mediocre army officer who had been chosen by the CIA to be its surrogate freedom fighter. Most historical accounts show that Castillo and his small band remained on the border of Honduras until the CIA had executed the coup in Guatemala City and forced Arbenz to seek asylum in an embassy. Then he was called in to take over as the Liberator. In the shadows was Mico Sandoval.

Before the era of firearms, war dogs were a major force in war. They terrorized infantry and could often be extremely effective against cavalry. The Celts had their dogs trained so that they would bite the noses of cavalry horses, causing them to throw their riders. This tactic was extremely important in neutralizing the Roman cavalry during the invasion of Britain.

　—Stanley Coren,
The Intelligence of Dogs: Canine Consciousness and Capabilities

While we waited for the great man to enter the sitting room, I had a flash of another story about monkeys and dogs that came from neighboring El Salvador, where I was based to cover the region's wars. That one concerned a terrifying army colonel who for a time had kept a monkey on a chain in his office. He would attempt to amuse visitors by crossing over a line painted on the floor, and then calling the monkey, who would scamper toward him and invariably get violently yanked by the neck leash that pulled taught just shy of the line. Such was the brand of humor we often dealt with in those heady days.

Later the Salvadoran colonel acquired a savage rottweiler that he loved dearly, and the monkey had disappeared. We never knew exactly what had happened, but he delighted in letting one believe that the dog had eaten the monkey.

That remembrance was suddenly interrupted by the entrance of The Godfather. El Mico. Don Mario Sandoval Alarcon.

Despite many years of interviewing varied personalities of Third World conflict, one finds that each encounter is different. As we settled into conversation, we found the aging Sandoval an oddly sympathetic figure, an anachronism not quite prepared for a changing world where the influence of Communism was already on the wane. His political party had already lost most of its power, as a neo-liberal political system of Christian Democrats and smooth-talkers of other more diplomatic right-wing movements had begun to take over.

Nevertheless, the old man was animated and lucid as he recounted his life's work, his virulent crusade. Perhaps it is like a marriage, where one has come to depend so much on one's life-long counterpart that it is inconceivable to live alone. Leftist student activists had long since ceased to study Marxist screeds very closely, but not him. At one point he proudly stated that his personal library of Communist literature was the most extensive of its kind in Latin America. He even gave us a tour of the vault, like the secret labyrinthine compartment of a medieval monastery.

The godfather was ensconced in his fortress, with his portrait of Castillo Armas; his library of Communist thought which he continued to study in profundity; and his memories of past glories.

It was the Autumn of the Patriarch, and I felt strangely sorry for him. Time was passing him by.

But he still had his other passion: his dogs. So we gravitated to that discussion, and he brought out examples of his prized breeds to display.

What sort of dog would be loved and bred by the man who was one of the most fearsome Latin legacies of the Cold War? Would they be flesh-eating pit bulls? Dobermans trained to tear Communists limb from limb? Rottweilers that ate leftists and Indians (but not monkeys)?

None of that.

This Mico's dogs were French poodles.

He sat on the sofa surrounded by four of his favorites, while I got to work photographing this unlikely scene. All the while these angry little tan poodles were growling in their fashion and yapping angrily at me, as if they knew I was not only an interloper, but also one reluctant to wholly embrace the household philosophy.

Attempting to get him to pose casually, I asked him about the particulars of breeding French poodles. What were the most important things to watch for? What were the pitfalls?

"*Cuesta que salgan blancos,*" he rasped through his throat hole. It's difficult to get them to come out white.

Thomas Long is a Central America-based correspondent and photographer for several U.S. and European publications. Since the mid-1980s, he has tracked and been tracked by varied species of tropical animals, four-legged and otherwise. He has been bitten more than once.

★

No one really knows where the Poodle originally came from. It almost certainly is not France, despite the fact the he is so often referred to as the French Poodle. It may have been Germany, although even that is doubtful.

The Poodle is one of the most intelligent of all dogs. He seems able to learn anything, and he makes a fine watchdog, and he is an excellent water retriever. The name Poodle is derived from the German slang word *pudelin*, which means, roughly, to splash around in the water.

The Poodle in his magnificent show clip is the brunt of many jokes, and the uninformed sometimes see it as an effete kind of status symbol. Were they to know! The Poodle in any clip is a superb dog—assertive, extremely responsive, loyal, and intelligent beyond belief.

—Roger Caras, *The Roger Caras Dog Book: A Complete Guide to Every AKC Breed*

D-L NELSON

Dogs' Night Out

*Two canines find a little patch of dog heaven
in a Heidelberg restaurant.*

"BRING THE BOYS," LLARA SAID. NORMALLY WHEN I VISITED HER
in Heidelberg, Germany, for a quality mother-daughter weekend,
my Japanese chins, Albert and Amadeus, were *canine non-grata*.

That was because of Waterloo, her rabbit. The first time the
boys and Waterloo met, the rabbit dived under the bed and spent
the rest of the weekend tapping out danger warnings to all the
non-existent bunnies in the building.

"What about Waterloo?" I asked.

"I got tired of her chewing everything." My daughter was talking on a new telephone. Waterloo had eaten her old one. "I found
a family that promised not to turn her into dinner."

Unlike in America, many public places happily accommodate
dogs. At the Café du Soleil, my favorite Geneva bistro and a regular stop for fondue, the owner welcomes them and always stops
are our table to say, "*Bonjour Albert. Bonjour Amadeus.*" Only afterwards does he add, "*Comment-allez vous Madame Nelson?*"

Last month when I was in the French Midi, I ducked into a
museum, half to escape the rain and half to look at the exhibit.

"We don't allow dogs," the cashier said, "but you can check
them with your raincoat and umbrella." When I returned from a

shortened visit, I found Amadeus playing with another checked dog and Albert asleep on the lap of the woman running the coat room.

So knowing travel and dogs presented no problem, I grabbed an overnight bag, their leashes, and passports. These are issued by my local vet and contain a complete shot record, although for all the years I've lived in Europe, I have never been asked to show them at a border crossing. Five hours of driving time later we pulled into a parking place in front of Llara's student apartment house.

After the normal greetings, my daughter, who claims cooking causes pimples, suggested we go out to dinner. Having eaten her attempts, I agreed.

We wandered through the old section of Heidelberg, looking into windows and admiring the lighted castle above. The dogs trotted along, leaving their marks at appropriate spots.

"Let's eat at the Kupfer Kanne," my daughter said. We had both dined there several times on earlier visits and had enjoyed the warmth both from the ceramic stove as we entered and the woman who we had guessed was the owner.

We were visiting two ladies in Brussels one time, and they took us out to dine at an elegant restaurant on Brussels's beautiful medieval square, the Grand Place. Our hostess took their little Belgian griffon along as a matter of course and the maître d'hôtel helped the dog into a chair at the table, so he could sit with the rest of us.

—Robert Scott Milne,
"Dogs Don't Lead a Dog's Life
in Europe"

We were never sure if her, "Nice to have you with us," was because she remembered us or because she was friendly.

"Is it okay to bring the dogs in?" My daughter asked in German, as the same woman, dressed in the traditional aproned dirndl, bustled up with menus in hand.

The woman looked down for the first time, turned on her heel, and led us to a small alcove off the main dining room. We'd never noticed it before. Ours was the only table, but it was set with the same linen as the others we'd passed and decorated with similar fresh daisies.

"Probably doesn't want anyone to see the dogs," my daughter said.

The boys settled in as we studied our menus. The woman reappeared and waited as we selected a white wine. I wanted trout. Llara chose pork chops. After taking our order, the woman listed what I took as the daily specials because I recognized the words for lamb and beef. It seemed strange to do that after we had ordered. My confusion didn't last long.

"She's naming dog food. She's going to feed the boys," Llara explained. "Is lamb okay for them?"

Within ten minutes all four of us were happily eating, the dogs at their usual vacuum-cleaner speed and Llara and I more slowly. The woman poked her head into the room and asked if the dogs wanted seconds.

"*Nein, danke,*" my daughter said.

After we finished the main course, Llara and I both gave in to apple strudel and espresso. The dogs were almost asleep when the owner brought the equivalent for them—a bowl of water and doggie candy.

As we finished our coffee, another couple who had been eating in the main room came by to meet the American dogs that the owner had told them about. Llara found herself answering the usual questions.

"No, they aren't related. One has English parents, the other has French."

"Fourteen and eight years old."

"They've flown the Atlantic eight times. In the baggage compartment. Without problems."

We ordered more coffee as the rest of the diners came in to say a few words and tell us about their animals. By 10:00 p.m. interest in the boys and us had waned, and we were finally alone.

"What do you think she'll charge for the dog food?" I asked as the woman disappeared to add up the costs.

Under the table Albert let out a long burp.

The woman returned, presented us the bill and opened the black money purse ubiquitous to all German waiters and waitresses. I scanned the numbers. Only the human meals were on it.

"*Fur die Hunden?*" I managed. The woman said something I didn't catch.

"She says they were her guests," my daughter translated.

From under the table, Albert burped again.

D-L Nelson is an American writer living in Geneva, Switzerland. She has had her short stories and articles published in four countries and is currently working on a Ph.D. in creative writing from the University of Lancaster, United Kingdom.

★

In the hills above Muenster, in French Alsace, we pulled off a country road at a sign marked *Ferme Auberge*. These farmhouses offer coffee, beer, and light lunches to travelers. Waiting at the door was a large black dog that seemed to have been out for a stroll. He went in with us; the farm wife smiled and nodded.

We ordered slabs of Muenster cheese with caraway seeds, and chucks of fresh French bread. The dog sprawled beneath our table. I realized that there was a dog at every table and travelers were trading stories about their beloved *chiens*.

When the gangly creature asleep on my foot was admired, I said, "He belongs to the farm." The farm wife smiled from the kitchen.

"No," she said. "I thought he was yours."

Everyone laughed at the clever interloper. No one suggested he leave. It's a dog's life in France, and *c'est bon*.

—Judith Morgan, "It's Definitely a Dog's Life in France"

PART THREE

SOME THINGS TO DO

ANN RAINCOCK

* * *

Sailing with Sam

How to "boat-break" a puppy
while living on the seven seas.

IT WAS THE CHILDREN, OF COURSE, WHO SAW IT—A CARD PINNED
up on a notice board in the little general store close to the harbor.
We were killing time, waiting for the aftermath of Hurricane Claus
to pass us by. Outside the fishing boats of Menemsha strained and
creaked on their lines, gray waves crashed over the harbor wall, and
the rain fell in slanting gusts. No boats would leave that day and an
afternoon confined to our own, while the rain beat on the decks
above and condensation dripped below, was not an appealing
prospect. I tried to gain some culinary inspiration from the meager
display of tinned foods while my husband flicked through the
store's magazines and the children read the cards on the wall.

"There's a notice over there." The younger one had appeared at
my side looking sheepish.

"What does it say?" I asked him.

"Golden retriever pups for sale."

Silence. He traced a design on the dusty floor with his damp
shoe. Then he took a deep breath.

"Can we buy one?"

I could hear his sister fidgeting from foot to foot in the aisle behind us, listening.

"No, my love," I laughed gently, putting my arm around his shoulders and drawing him towards me. "That really wouldn't be a good idea—not under the circumstances."

"The children saw an advertisement for golden retriever pups back in the store," I said quietly to my husband later. The children were in the aft cabin reading. "What do you think?"

"What do I think?" he echoed in amazement. "Are you crazy? Here are four of us confined to a sail boat, over a year of traveling still ahead of us, and you want a dog—a puppy? He'd need training, and walks, and visits to the vet, and bags of food, and bowls, and…and…." he sputtered to a halt, catching his breath before continuing. "You must be out of your mind…all of you…no…absolutely, definitely no!" His raised voice had brought the children from their cabin.

Four hours later we wrote a check and received in return a small, warm, furry bundle with bright eyes and a black, wet nose. He had been born in Washington D.C. nearly seven weeks earlier and his owners had brought him, along with his brother, sister, and mother, to their summer home on Martha's Vineyard, hoping to sell the puppies there. After our telephone call they had immediately driven the dogs to the general store near the harbor to meet us. We had huddled out of the rain under the porch talking while the children had sat, speechless with excitement, on the old seat outside the store with the three puppies wriggling on their laps.

"Which one is it to be?" their father had asked.

Our daughter had shrugged her shoulders, eyes wide. This was no time to get into an argument with her more opinionated brother; everything at this meeting must run smoothly.

"This one," said her brother firmly, indicating the darker male. "Definitely this one."

And so he came with us. He was destined to grow up on a sail boat and to travel over 6,000 miles in the first year of his life. And he was destined, too, to change our lives and to bring a new dimension to our long-planned sailing adventure. But first, on that blustery afternoon, we took him on board and showed him his new home. Then we put a cushion in a corner of the main cabin where he promptly fell asleep, while the children settled down to watch him for hours until he awoke. While he slept we talked quietly and decided to call him Sam; Sailor Sam.

By the next morning the wind had diminished and the Sound was calmer; it was time to leave. We maneuvered out of our dock and set sail for Newport, Rhode Island, with Sam snuggled against the breeze on one lap or another. The pattern of that day was to repeat itself often in the days to come as we criss-crossed the Sound on our journey back to New York, before heading south for a year. For Sam, each day presented a new challenge: climbing on board from a variety of docks, scrambling out of the cockpit onto the deck, disentangling himself from a bundle of lines inadvertently dropped on him, and negotiating the steep steps of the companionway to the safety of "down below." When at anchor we used an inflatable dinghy to go ashore. Of course while small he could be lifted and passed down and up again, but the day would come when he'd have to jump. And jump he did, as soon as he was able.

The decision of when to let him take his first swim was made for us when, eager to reach the beach, he mistimed his disembarkation from the dinghy and flung himself into the water. He was to swim almost every day of the trip from then on, becoming strong and powerful and able to keep his head underwater for considerable periods of time while attempting to retrieve a stone or some other interesting item from the bottom.

A "dogwatch" is a nautical term referring to the two-hour watches (4-6 p.m. and 6-8 p.m.), instead of the usual four-hour watches, introduced to enable seamen to vary their daily watch-keeping rota. Among various suggested origins are that it is a "docked" or shortened watch.

—Brewer's Dictionary of Phrase and Fable

That first summer of our trip was drawing to a close as we motored down the East River, past Manhattan's Battery Point and turned to the south. By now Sam was well trained and well accustomed to the cruising life. Except on rare occasions we stopped every night, anchoring in a quiet bay or taking a berth at a marina.

Then, in fair weather or foul, we would ride ashore in the dinghy or disembark on the dock to take him for a walk, discovering many delights which we might otherwise have missed had we stayed on board. When we were late, and conscious that he might be uncomfortable, we would try to encourage him to relieve himself on deck (where a quick bucket of water would have taken care of the clean-up) but he never would and we respected him for that.

As the fall months passed we made our way down the eastern seaboard. We found a vet in Maryland for the necessary shots and a check up and everywhere we went we made new friends. He was a great conversation starter; all the people we met, whether ashore or on other boats, wanted to know how we had acquired Sam. And he was good, oh so very good. When we rented a car and took the children to Washington he thought this novel mode of transportation a great treat. And when we left him to sleep soundly on the back seat while we visited some museums there he patiently complied. He was a quiet dog, not stirring in the morning until someone in the family did, and rarely barking unless to encourage the dolphins that would soon come and play in our wake as we traveled through the Carolinas and beyond. Although very active, he also loved to sit beside the children, head on lap or sandy feet, while the obligatory school work was done and in this way he helped to curb the children's restlessness.

We crossed the Gulf Stream from Fort Lauderdale to the Bahamas two days before Christmas and would not leave that island nation for five months. There Sam came to believe that life was, indeed, a beach. There he would swim and dive and run, or engage in his ongoing project—always interrupted by his family impatient to move on—of digging a hole to Australia. But life was not always perfect. One day, as we splashed through the shallows at Green Turtle Key in the Abacos searching for shells, a dark object swimming nearby caught Sam's attention. The young stingray darted away with Sam in hot pursuit and all the shouting and whistling in the world would have been to no avail. As we ran we watched in horror as Sam reached his prey. For what seemed like a very long time, but was probably only seconds, we witnessed the golden dog and the writhing gray wings come together, jumping, twisting, and thrashing in showers of silver spray. Then the ray hit his target and was gone. Sam yelped and lay down in the shallow water, examining his foreleg in confusion. He had only wanted to play. When we reached him we discovered he had been hit; the ray's barbed "sting" was firmly embedded in his leg. There was no other course of action available to us; without benefit of professional medical help the sting would have to be pushed through the leg and removed from the other side. So that is what we did. He bore it stoically and soon we were carrying him across the sun-dappled shallows with heavy hearts. Had muscles or tendons been severed? Would he suffer permanent damage? How could we prevent the wound from becoming infected? We were relieved that he had not been hit more horribly—in the head or, worse, the eye—but we were worried nonetheless. Yet his recovery was swift. He licked the wound himself and it quickly healed, leaving no discernible damage to the leg. My daughter still has the barbed sting, kept carefully in a tiny box among her shell collection.

Together we shared many hours of pure perfection and a few hours of grave concern. Once, on encountering an unexpected storm on the Bahama bank, my husband indicated to me that he would like the children to be below. "I don't like Sam being up here in this very rough weather," I was able to say to them. "Why don't you both go and snuggle up in the V-berth and keep him safe and calm until we're through this bad weather?"

All too soon we had to plan our return; our adventure was coming to an end and, fourteen months after our departure, we were to return to our urban life in Toronto, Canada. Another new world was waiting for Sam: the cold and snow of a northern winter, sleeping in a house, walking in a busy street, and being confined to a garden where he was not allowed to try digging to Australia.

Today, nearly twelve years after that wet windy afternoon on Martha's Vineyard, Sam is still with us. The children are grown-up now and much has changed, but every summer we all move aboard the boat docked on Toronto Islands. There Sam passes lazy days watching the ducks and snoozing on deck in the sun, waiting for us to return from our various daily activities. We call "Yo, Sailor Sam," as we approach and then he stirs, stretches and comes, tail wagging, to the bow to greet us and we know he is happy; this really is his home. For early every Spring, when the snow has nearly gone and the days are getting longer, Sam becomes uncharacteristically restless. Then we put him in the car and drive down to the still-icy lake and show him the old boat and tell him that summer is coming.

Ann Raincock is a British Canadian travel writer and editor of Travel-Scoop. *She currently lives in Toronto from where, every summer, she and her family sail their ketch* SuperRooster *on Lake Ontario.*

★

In the first week of September, my father announced that he and I and Mutt would take the vessel [*Scotch Bonnet*] down the lake to the Bay of Quinte. The storm warnings were flying and the seas, running in across some 40 miles of open water, were thundering against the concrete barriers along the shore.

We had no sooner cleared Toronto Island than we saw a strange spectacle ahead. It looked at first as if a drunken forest was staggering toward us out of the storm darkness.

"Look," my father whooped joyfully. "That's the cross-lake race from Rochester...the yachting boys...and they're running for shelter under bare poles."

We drove through that battered fleet like another *Flying Dutchman*. It was an exhilarating moment, but when we had come about and were beating eastward down the coast, I remembered that I had not seen Mutt for half an hour. I went below to seek him.

I found him on my bunk, up forward of the mainmast, where the motion was the worst. He was stretched at full length, his head on my pillow and his feet hanging limply over the side of the bunk. He looked as if he believed, and hoped, that he was already dead. He took no notice of my arrival except to roll his eyes until the sight of those bloodshot orbs made me think suddenly of my own stomach, and I hastened out on deck again.

I told my father that Mutt was dying.

"He'll get over it," my father said.

And of course he did. By the next dawn he was up and around again; but in future when the storm warnings were flying he never showed quite the same enthusiasm for sailing that had been his on that first day we went to sea.

—Farley Mowat, *The Dog Who Wouldn't Be*

SUSAN ALLEN TOTH

Sheepdog Trials: A Field Trip

*An American couple learn the finer points
about one of England's most popular
competitive sports.*

SHEEPDOG TRIALS—LEWES—SAT, JULY 21. ALTHOUGH IT WAS only a crudely painted sign stuck on a roadside fence, it caught my attention. As my husband James and I had tramped around the English and Welsh countryside over the years, we'd sometimes watched in admiration as a small black-and-white dog in a nearby pasture moved a flock of sheep across a field and through a gate. I had only a vague image of sheepdog trials, but a few days before, I'd tuned into the last minutes of a BBC television program called *One Man and His Dog.* Its chatty host was interviewing a taciturn man in mud-spattered clothes standing next to an intelligent-looking, bright-eyed sheepdog. They were talking about a trial the dog had just won. I wished I'd been able to see the man and his dog in action.

At the time, I assumed that the program featured different dog stories each week—perhaps a champion Jack Russell, a corgi related to Queen Elizabeth's, or a Labrador who'd recently saved a baby from a burning house. I did not know that sheepdog trials were a popular competitive sport with regular regional meets, national champions, and international contests, nor could I have guessed that such trials provided weekly tension-filled moments for a popular T.V. show.

I was about to learn. It was not easy to find the Lewes Sheepdog Trials, even though an accommodating hotel clerk had telephoned the Lewes Tourist Information Agency and learned that the trials began at nine a.m. Sunday at Deans Farm on the Puddingham Road. She wasn't quite sure about Puddingham. Neither were we. But if the trials were a major event, we'd be sure to find it, perhaps on a public parade ground or soccer field outside Lewes, a thriving market town not far from Brighton.

After [many miles and wrong turns,] we rounded a curve and emerged onto the top of the ridge. There, just in front of us, clustered in front of a gate, were several young girls in what looked like scouts' uniforms and an older man sitting on a portable chair. One of the girls held a large roll of tickets. They were the first people we'd seen since we left the main road from Lewes. I looked beyond the gate. Far below, in the bottom of a broad shallow basin of green grass that swooped up to the sky, I could see what must be the sheepdog trials.

No bleachers. No crowds. Only vast green fields, a square of golden wheat on one far horizon, three or four windblown trees on another, lots of blue sky. Strung in an odd-looking straight line across the valley floor were perhaps two dozen cars, mostly station wagons, vans, and hatchbacks with their trunk lids flung up. Behind the cars stood a large tent and a white semitrailer truck with a sign on it. I kept my eyes on this rigid line of bright cars, an incongruous slash in the green flowing landscape, as we bumped slowly down a precipitous path to the valley floor. There, at a gap in the fence, standing guard near a pair of portable toilet cubicles, another uniformed girl took our ticket and waved toward the grass.

As we slowly rolled across the field to the cars, I could now read the semi's cheerful logo: DI'S FARMHOUSE KITCHEN. A flap in its side had been opened to form a shelf. Tea, I thought comfortably. Scones, freshly cut sandwiches, cake. Ah, the English. As we passed the tent I noticed many empty tables set up beneath it. If a crowd ever arrived, the organizers of the Lewes Charity Sheepdog Trials were certainly prepared.

A few people were standing by their cars or sitting on folding chairs, two or three walking from one car to another. Most were looking at the field where, just barely visible in the distance, a small black-and-white shape was moving down the valley, not far from a cluster of other, slightly larger, white shapes. We pulled up in an empty space in the line, slowly and quietly, careful not to slam the car door as we got out. Next to us two border collies were tethered to a temporary fence between the cars and the field. They, too, were watching the valley intently.

> *The border collie's natural herding instinct allows it to handle up to several hundred sheep alone, primarily by means of a mesmerizing stare known as the "eye."*
>
> —Jon Winokur, *Mondo Canine*

Directly ahead of us in the field was a gatelike structure, two sections of wooden fence forming a wide opening, and on either side were two identical structures. These gates were clearly the obstacles, but what was the dog supposed to do? Where were the sheep supposed to go? To our right was a wooden circular pen, just large enough to hold a half-dozen sheep. Now I noticed a man standing in the field not far from the pen, whistling loudly through cupped hands. Then he shouted a series of commands I couldn't follow. The dog dashed to and fro, the sheep hurried this way and that. They seemed as confused as I was.

"The program explains it," James said helpfully, handing me the printed handout he'd gotten at the hilltop gate. I tried to read it quickly, following a sketch of a typical course and matching what I read to what was going on here—or *not* going on, since the man and his dog had just abruptly left the field, disappearing behind the line of cars. The sheep milled aimlessly.

"Too bad," said another man, leaning on the hood of the van next to us, to a woman behind the wheel. "Sam just wouldn't stop for him." I decided to ask for help. Though the English have a reputation for reticence, I have seldom failed to have my inquiries answered with full and polite instruction. They usually like to educate ignorant but well-meaning Americans.

"Excuse me," I said. "Would you be kind enough to tell me why that man took his dog off the field so suddenly? Did something go wrong?"

"Lost too many points. He knew he didn't stand a chance," the man answered. He pointed to the program in my hand. "It explains it all in there."

"I know, but I don't seem to quite follow everything," I admitted. "This is the first time I've been to a sheepdog trial."

He stood up and walked over to us. "Now, see," he said, waving toward the field, "there's a maximum of twenty points on the fetch." He began to describe each section of the trial, growing more enthusiastic and voluble as he went on. In a few minutes, another man joined him, adding his own comments and explanations. James and I listened carefully. Gradually I began to understand what they were telling us.

At the beginning of each trial, the competitor stands with his or her dog at a post just beyond the temporary fence. Over a loudspeaker, an announcer calls both names, equal billing for dog and handler: "Next, Robert Stephenson with Moss," or "Douglas Parkins with Jet." All the dogs at Lewes had one-syllable names, sturdy and straightforward: Dan, Sweep, Ben, Roy.

One of the judges waves a flag—here at Lewes, it was a makeshift cloth tied to a long-handled black umbrella—toward the far end of the field. There, so far away I could only make out their white shapes by squinting, another official releases five sheep from a holding pen. At a hand signal from his owner, the dog sets out to retrieve the sheep.

When a sheepdog leaves the post, he begins his *outrun*, the first phase of the trial. (Each phase has an optimum number of possible points that can be awarded.) To avoid coming at the sheep head-on, and alarming or scattering them, the dog circles widely to the right or left, an approach that is ideally pear-shaped. When the dog contacts the sheep, he has completed his second phase, the *lift*. Now he must drive the little flock back toward his handler.

The first sheepdog trials were held in 1873 in Wales. Ten dogs competed.

—CH

Watching the eager border collies streak up the field, James and I could scarcely believe their speed. Crouching low, a black-and-white blur in the tall grass, a dog usually reached the end of the field in moments. "Oh yes," our neighbor assured us, "he can get up to forty miles an hour, can a good dog." Speed is not the only consideration, however. In the third phase, the *fetch*, as the dog brings the sheep down the field, he is supposed to herd them in a straight line. But sheep do not like straight lines. They have their own ideas.

Nor do they have any desire to cooperate in the *drive*, the next phase, a triangular course that passes through two gate obstacles. The dog is supposed to move, turn, and keep the sheep in line without upsetting them. As with people, I gathered, it was better to nudge, suggest, and persuade rather than to intimidate. Yet sheep have the irritating habit of bolting this way or that, separating from the flock without warning, or turning at the last possible moment to skirt a gate. And some sheep, our neighbor told us, are simply a bad lot. "Occasionally you get a rogue. Real trouble. Not much you can do about it."

In the final two phases of the trial, the *shed* and *pen*, the dog has to perform even more intricate maneuvers. First, at a signal, the dog must identify two sheep specially marked by large collars and then cut them off from the flock. Finally, after again collecting the sheep, the dog is supposed to herd them into the pen. The sheep do not tend to file into the pen without a fuss. The handler, standing at the gate of the pen and holding it open, can wave his shepherd's staff and try to block the meandering sheep with his body, but he or she cannot let go of the gate. Too many shouts, gestures, and stick brandishings cost points.

During the trial, the handler uses several kinds of signals. To James and me, novices in the art of sheep herding, the most intriguing was the whistle. Holding his hand cupped before his mouth, sometimes the handler almost seemed to be playing a virtuoso instrument, varying in pitch and tone. Some handlers used a mechanical whistle, others depended only on their own innate skill. As the piercing, rolling trill rang out over the field, the dog seemed to hear its notes like a private musical language. All James and I caught was its urgency.

Once, when a particularly recalcitrant sheep had broken from its fellows and bolted for the third time, a frustrated dog lost its control, snapped at the sheep, and seized it by the wool at its neck. Grabbing a sheep was a severe fault, costing the dog's handler many points.

After giving us basic instructions, our neighbor returned to his absorbed perch on his van. Before long, it would be his turn. Almost all the spectators were also competitors.

"How long will the trials go on?" I'd asked him, still worrying we might have missed too much.

"Oh, all day," he'd said casually. "Sometimes the judges don't post any ratings until the very end, so we all have to hang around till six or seven."

Now I understood why Di's Farmhouse Kitchen had settled for the day behind the parked cars. James and I wandered over to its window to buy ourselves some tea and cake.

As the morning deepened, so did our interest. Although we could not judge the finer points, we could follow the basic maneuvers. For me, it was rather like watching baseball: I can cheer strikeouts and home runs, but I don't notice a batter's stance at the plate or the spin on a pitcher's fastball. Watching sheepdogs, I did not know why one managed to pen its flock on the first try—and why others never managed it at all.

James and I realized that most successful handlers used the fewest signals. If properly trained, a dog understood immediately what he was supposed to do and required little further guidance.

Sometimes, however, a dog in a difficult situation had to check with its handler constantly. Then, while continuing to stare down the restless sheep, the dog had to follow a series of rapid-fire signals—"Move!" "Stop!" "Stand!" "Keep quiet!" "Hunker down!" "Move!"—and react with precision timing.

As we understood more, our tension mounted: I found myself straining to see the faraway lift and assess the fetch. Soon we knew when a dog had a bad start, running too directly (not in the recommended pear shape) toward the waiting sheep. When the sheep swept too fast down the field, rushing past the first gate obstacle before the dog could turn them, we realized his handler was in trouble. We waited with bated breath as a dog almost drove the sheep into the pen—and then missed, as one sheep bolted and dashed away, distracting the dog's attention from the rest of the flock, who then hurried off to the edge of the field.

Our hearts went out to both dog and owner. Each time a dog took its place at the post, we wanted him and his owner to do well.

The other man who'd earlier helped us understand what was happening walked by. "Enjoying it, are you?" he inquired pleasantly.

"Oh yes," I said, adding, to prolong the conversation, "and now when I watch *One Man and His Dog,* I'll know what's happening."

I couldn't have made a less propitious remark. His face darkened, and for a moment I thought he was going to spit, if not at me, at least in the general direction of my unwitting idiocy. "*Television,*" he said with great emphasis. "You can't think that *television* show has anything to do with a real sheepdog trial. Bloody deceptive, that's what that is. And I say that even though I'm going to be on it in a few weeks myself. Oh yes. Why, they spend ten, twelve hours just getting the camera angle set up, in the hills, or on the fence, or maybe even in the trees. Sometimes they build a tower just to put a camera in so they can look down the field for the proper close-up or stare into a dog's eyes. Close-ups, that's all they care about. And then all that folderol about the dog and its owner. Pat your dog on the head for the camera." He looked again as if he would like to spit. "No, don't tell me about *television.*" He waved at the field. "Now this," he said with emphasis, "*this* is the real thing."

I followed his wave. It took in the deep valley, its green billowing grass spotted with red poppies; the silence, broken only by the low murmur of the onlookers, the handler's whistle and shouted commands that were almost lost on the wind; the blue sky with huge white clouds, the sea just over the downs, the clear clean air, the sense of remoteness, the absolute sweep of it all.

Toward noon, James and I consulted. We had only watched about a third of the trials, but we had promised ourselves a walk along the sea. This was the only day we'd be able to get to the coast. So regretfully, we climbed back into our car, as quietly as possible, not wanting our neighbor to notice our early departure, and timing it so that the current sheepdog would be at the far end of the field. I was sorry we couldn't stay to see his fetch.

Susan Allen Toth is a graduate of Smith College, the University of California at Berkeley, and the University of Minnesota, where she received her Ph.D. Currently a professor of English at Macalester College in St. Paul, Minnesota, she is a committed Anglophile and has written extensively about England. This story is excerpted from her book, My Love Affair with England.

✷

"It's funny, mention sheepdog trials and people instantly think that all the participants are cockeys," said Wayne Mathieson. "But nothing could be further from the truth. We're not all workers on the land. We've got a mix of accountants, jewelers, office workers, shearers—you name a profession and chances are we've got one of them here. And the best part about it is that everyone gets on. We're lucky. In sheepdog trials we don't have that bitchiness you tend to get in other sports. Everyone just has a great time."

—Michael Cowley, "Sheepdog Trials: OK, Babe, Try to Match This,"
Sydney Morning Herald

LOUISE RAFKIN

The Things We Do for Love

*Without her Labrador by her side, the author learns
that money can't buy you puppy love.*

I RARELY GO ANYWHERE WITHOUT MY DOG. SHE'S NOT SMALL AND it's not always easy, but I travel a lot and she accompanies me, taking in business lunches and social engagements as easily as trips to the park. She herself travels well, and appreciates both city and country. Most importantly, no matter where I am, if she is with me, I don't feel lonely. But I couldn't take her to Japan.

So there I was in Tokyo, staying right next to a park where each morning streams of morning dog walkers came to stroll under the picturesque maples. For the first few days I soothed my dog cravings simply by setting myself on a bench and smiling at passing pooches. The medium-sized Japanese breeds—the fox-like Hokkaidoken, Akita inu, and the shiba—were, of course, highly represented. Yet most of the dogs were small (due no doubt to Tokyo's postage stamp housing), well groomed, and generally well behaved. I did see one hefty German shepherd, caught up in the chase of a golden-eyed duck, take his tiny owner for a spin, and eventually a spill. There wasn't the socializing between owners like we have stateside, but owners nodded to each other as they made their daily rounds. Poop scooping was *de rigueur*, fastidiously executed like only the hyper-clean Japanese would manage, with tiny shovels and rakes.

I mooned over several delightful Pekingese, and one afternoon helped a dachshund disentangle itself from its owner. But after of a week of doglessness I was desperate. The largeness and foreignness of Japan had mixed in me to create a faint homesickness, and I missed my pet. I had read a news item about Tokyo pet shops that offer rent-a-dogs. I set off to find a myself a companion for the lovely afternoon, determined to assuage any creeping loneliness with the simple act of dog bonding.

I dragged a Japanese-speaking expatriate along for the adventure. Heidi had never heard about Tokyo rental dogs and was sure it was a cultural myth. ("Like internal deodorant," she commented. Apparently a popular newspaper reported that pill deodorant is the rage in America and now she is routinely asked if she eats her deodorant.) Thoroughly unconvinced, she nevertheless marched around with me to several pet shops. At each, we were met with blank stares, shrugs, and several looks that translated, I suspect, as "crazy Americans."

Undaunted, I snagged the phone book. And there it was—sort of. The ad for the upscale pet shop seemed to suggest that the dogs were available. I made Heidi call to verify the situation. We learned that yes, this was an actual rental shop and yes, dogs were standing by this very afternoon! The pet shop was located in a wealthy suburb, several trains and trams from the busy shopping area in which I was staying.

"What are we doing?" Heidi asked as we turned the corner and heard the cacophony of barking.

A golden lab about the size of my own beloved met us at the door. Several miniature Shih-Tzus beckoned from inside their cages. Dachshunds peered up from their hutch, and a bundle of poodle pups somersaulted in their crib. Dogs! My heart filled. Heidi went to negotiate the deal. The lab attached itself to my leg. I petted and patted, and soon she rolled belly up, paws in the air and brown eyes locked to mine.

"Five thousand yen for a big dog and three thousand for a small one," Heidi reported, rolling her eyes. "Until six." It was already after three. More conversing revealed that the afternoon rate period had already kicked in, and we wouldn't get a break for our late start.

I stood deliberating in front of the bank of caged smaller pups, but the lab would have none of it. She nuzzled my backside, whined, and licked my hands. She was indeed quite sweet. Those eyes! I shrugged. "What's a few more yen?" I handed over the whopping fee, about twenty-five dollars per hour, and received a leash, several baggies, and some toilet tissues in return. The dog realized it had me snared and leapt in joy. I clicked the leash on and was immediately dragged towards the door.

"Its name," I said, trying to control the suddenly not so docile beast. "Find out her name!"

"Rub," said the pretty Japanese clerk, belying some understanding of English.

"Rub?" we asked. She nodded. A volley of Japanese exchanged, but by this time Rub had led me halfway down the street.

"Love," Heidi explained when she finally caught up. A language teacher, Heidi finally realized the clerk was having difficulty with English consonants. Rub's actual name was "Love."

"No, Love! No!" I tried to resist being dragged into a garbage heap. Love made for a smelly fish head. I wrestled Love away. I'm fairly good with dogs, but this one had its own mind. And she did not respond to any of the pronunciations of her name. Rub, Ruv, or Love, it didn't much matter.

A couple of Caucasians with an unruly dog raised some eyebrows, and even elicited smiles from the usually stoic locals. According to our map, there was a park not far from the pet shop. We questioned several passersby, most who remarked that the park was straight ahead but much too far away to walk to. As the Japanese are notoriously poor pedestrians, we kept to our course.

Love, weaving in and out of doorways, and alternating between pulling and stopping every other second for bursts of intense sniffing, led us haltingly towards the park. When stopped, I couldn't

budge her. I tried all my dog-training voices, high, low, command-
ing, and firm. I tried to establish eye contact but she would have
nothing of it. I pleaded and wheedled, a dog-training no-no, but it
was absolutely clear that it was Love who had us by the lead.

Finally reaching the park, we encountered other dog owners
and participated in that particular interaction in which dogs sniff
each others' hindquarters while owners smile and nod. Even cross-
culturally and with the language barrier, I enjoyed this part of what
by this point was beginning to feel like an ordeal.

As darkness began to fall, we headed back. Enough Love is
enough. But Love didn't appreciate us cutting her session short,
and the trek back to the shop was more like a battle of tug-o-war.
I tried handing off the leash to Heidi.

"No way," she said. "I'm just the translator."

"Tell her to come then," I begged. Heidi barked something
Love's way.

"Maybe my accent's not that good," she quipped.

And just then Love got us in some real trouble. While waiting
for a light to change, Love leaned over and sniffed the crotch of an
elderly man. He jumped back and let out a scream loud and high
enough to bring shop owners to their doors. And then he let us
have it, a spew of angry sound, emitted from a face contorted into
a lemon squeeze. Heidi translated a few words, something about a
fear of dogs and horrible foreigners, before she crossed the street,
fleeing in embarrassment. I bowed repeatedly, said I was sorry, and
looked around to find Love, oblivious, scarfing up something
unidentifiable.

Dropping Love at the shop was uneventful. She skipped off towards her kennel mates, no doubt to gloat over the details of her
excursion. I called to her and knelt down and attempted some eye-
to-eye contact, but our deal was over and Love wouldn't play act
some meaningful goodbye. At one point I turned around and she
bit my sweater, no doubt her final comment on our relationship.

Back on the street, night had fallen over Tokyo and walls of
neon lights blared from outside our train. I felt sad and empty inside. For the first time I understood a man's compulsion to visit a

prostitute. I felt like I had joined the ranks of such men. Far from home, I was lonely and missed my true love. I thought I could buy some affection, but as it turned out, Love couldn't be bought.

And no, I haven't yet told my dog.

Louise Rafkin, author of many books including the forthcoming What Do Dogs Dream? *(Andrews & McMeel), is best known as stage mother of Lucy, a lab-mix, who has aspirations for Hollywood. To this end, Lucy has learned to jump through hoops—literally.*

★

The man in God's Kritturs was tending a bank of illuminated aquariums. "You want to…borrow…a dog. For a…month." He straightened up and turned around to face me.

Well, I thought more like—rent."

"Rent-a-Dawg."

"I've got a spook caller, in the small hours…"

He smiled patiently. In the pet shop business, you get to meet all kinds of crazy people. "'Fraid I just can't help you there," he said. "But if a Siamese fighting fish was any good to you…"

William the pharmacist suggested the dog pound at the Animal Hospital on Henry Street, where I raised only a faint zephyr of amusement ("Gentlemen here wants a tempo-rary, re-turnable dog") and was shown to the cells at the back of the building. The dogs were short of ears, eyes, fur, and teeth. They had the resigned manners of long-term detainees. Some slept, whiffling asthmatically; some raised a single bored eye as I peered at them through the wire. One growled, but it was a countertenor, not a bass.

A technician came over to say, "You looking to borrow a dog? I got a dog you can borrow if you want." She occupied every available inch of an outsize t-shirt that asked HAVE YOU HUGGED YOUR HORSE TODAY? "She's a black lab, she's trained. She's old, but she still barks real good at strangers in the night."

"And she won't mind?"

"Gypsy? No, she'll just mooch all the love out of you she can. She's a big love-dog."

"Won't you miss her?"

I got more dogs out at my place 'n I can keep a count of. You want to borrow my dog, you're most welcome."

—Jonathan Raban, *Hunting Mister Heartbreak*

BRIAN PATRICK DUGGAN

★ ☆ ★

The Dog Who Wasn't
Supposed to Go

Come behind the scenes at a dog show
and watch the fur fly.

IT PROBABLY STARTED WITH THE BED SHEETS THAT LOOKED LIKE A bunch of pastel mints. I should have realized then and there that there were going to be certain decisions in the marriage that I was just not going to make. That was how I came to be sitting in the San Francisco airport bound for Lexington, Kentucky, with some fairly unusual luggage and four dogs, wondering if the small wire cutters and multi-tool in my fanny-pack were going to earn me a strip search at the security check-point.

The Saluki Club of America National Specialty is the biggest Saluki show in the States and possibly the world. It is a prestigious event and my wife, Wendy, declared that for our hounds' debut, we must do it right. Doing it right meant the best of our breeding proudly exhibited. "Fine by me, which two are we taking?"

"Well, actually we are taking four." She detailed to me the classes that the dogs would compete in to make the proper showing. Our exquisite Miqa, her two sons Djaaz and Djinn, and her grandson, Ziir, were all required. Thinking that Ziir at barely a year old, was too young to be competitive, I suggested three dogs as a compromise. No, Ziir was particularly required for the puppy sweepstakes. Wendy said the compromise was *only* taking four dogs, pointing out that it could have been more (a bluff as it turned out—the airlines limit two dogs per passenger). Bulldozed by the inescapable logic, I gave in—Ziir would go.

The Kentucky State Horse Park is a stud farm and monument to the American thoroughbred race horse. Dominating the horizon around the visitor center is a huge bronze statue of Man o' War. Sculptures and exhibits pay homage to all breeds—from the mighty Belgian draft horse to the hairy Shetland pony. Once a year, the Horse Park hosts "The Egyptian Event" a world-class Arabian horse show and exhibition. Marking the connection between two noble animals from the Middle East, the Saluki National Specialty is held on the grounds and Salukis are welcome to visit the horses, vendors, and arena.

Now, location at a dog show is very important. Shade is highly desirable but you also want a clear view of the competition. And you want to sit close to your friends but away from *those* people. After setting up, our dogs were content to languidly observe the proceedings or stretch out and sleep in their pen. Presumably they were as jet-lagged as we were after the red-eye flight, but since they sleep about eighteen hours a day anyway it was hard to detect a difference.

Dog show judging is kind of like trying to decide who would be the best pole vaulter by watching the athletes trot in a circle and squeezing their muscles. Judges must make an informed decision based on their experience and knowledge without actually letting the dogs do their particular specialty. Unlike other sporting events, once you have entered the ring with your dog, the outcome is entirely up to the judge. Athletes can beat their competitors by swimming faster, jumping higher, or shooting straighter. But, assuming your dog is moderately well behaved in the ring, you cannot really do anything to influence the outcome—although some dog handlers feel that additional effort is needed to help the judge decide correctly.

Handler's tricks can range from benign, such as stacking your dog (standing him four-square for examination) a little closer to the judge to make him stand out in the line up—to downright malignant and deliberate attempts to distract and interfere with other dogs or actually intimidate the judge. However, some tactics are just legitimate showmanship, like making sure that your dog is not obscured by a tent pole or setting up a dark coated dog in the sun rather than the shade to highlight her coat and musculature.

There were 479 Salukis entered and a variety of activities to spread the event over three days. The sole source of food, a pathetic hot dog cart, compelled the discerning to bring deli sandwiches or send out for fast food. One morning, a "Bedouin Brunch" was held but it was plain that it was neither Bedouin food nor made by a Bedouin. We watched the judging, visited

The exotic Saluki may be the oldest breed of purebred dog in the world. Some people insist he is the dog the Sumerians knew and used almost seven thousand years before Christ—which would make him almost nine thousand years old.

—Roger Caras, The Roger Caras Dog Book: A Complete Guide to Every AKC Breed

with friends, shopped for doggy supplies and Saluki trinkets. Vendors at dog shows offer a bewildering array of enhancing shampoos, conditioners, treatments, and powders, all sold to help your dog win. The amount of trimming, brushing, polishing, fluffing, and general fussiness depends on the individual breed and type of coat, and I have seen freshly groomed dogs carried through the dog show with all the care of a junior auction assistant handling a Ming vase at Sotheby's.

Salukis were bred for hunting gazelle and hare in the desert and are supposed to be shown *au natural*. A quick brush through their ear and tail feathering is all that is needed. Some Saluki owners get really protective of this ornamentation and despite the heat and humidity of Kentucky in June, we saw a few bag-heads at ringside with cloth "snoods," designed to pull their ears up out of harm's way. The heat was such that clothes were drenched with sweat twenty minutes after arriving at the show and shade for both humans and canines was paramount. Even under our umbrellas and sheets we used water soaked terry cloth coats and a spray bottle to kept the dogs comfortable.

Our judge from New Zealand was familiar with American ring procedure and selected an unconventional but effective way of evaluating the dogs. Normally, an exhibitor will "stack" the dog. Some handlers will try to hide cow-hocked hindquarters or sagging toplines by careful over-corrections of the dog's stance or artful pressure with a prodding finger. This particular judge asked each exhibitor to walk their dog a few paces forward, breaking the meticulous stack and allowing the dog to stand naturally. In showing dogs, you are supposed to do what the judge tells you. I quickly adapted and it was no problem to show Ziir that way—he is dead sound, stacked or not. Some competitors just couldn't resist fussing with their dogs even after being told to let them stand naturally. So they had to do it over. Ziir and I had fun, and did just fine. The temperature and humidity were oppressive and with no breeze, the dogs needed careful watching to see that they did not overheat. Large buckets of ice water were made available for dousing the hounds and our judge announced that she did not care if they were soaking wet when she examined them. So much for the meticulous grooming and fluffy feathering.

There are odd-sounding categories of competition—American Bred, Novice, Open, and Bred by Exhibitor—which are confusing to the neophyte. We were floored when the dark red Ziir won the blue ribbon in the Twelve-to-Eighteen-Month class. (Wendy had asked me if I wanted something to do, like taking Ziir in the ring. "Sure. Why not?") Pretty good for a youngster who had just turned a year old against dogs that had up to six months more maturity and development! Djaaz, a black-fringed red and Djinn, a fawn and white parti-color, looked good but did not place in their classes. Ziir's win elated Wendy and we thought that he might have a shot at Reserve Winners. But no one was more surprised than I when the judge later pointed out young Ziir as Winner's Dog (best non-champion male). The next day, Saturday, was the competition for the bitches and Miqa took third place in Veteran Bitch (females over seven years old). On Sunday, Ziir went back into competition with the champions for Best of Breed. We were on a fantastic high at that point—who would have thought it? Our flight home was at 5 p.m. on Sunday—we hadn't expected to get that far in the competition and had planned to leave early. Ziir's win meant that we would have to trade the flight for the final round. We canceled our reservations—after all we didn't come all that way to sight-see.

In stifling heat and in stiff competition with 110 champions, the Finnish dog that won Winners Bitch took Best of Breed and the judge then gave Ziir Best of Opposite Sex, which meant that he had bested all the champion males. Wendy just about exploded and I was in a daze. Ziir knew that something good had happened, but he wasn't sure what. The triumph was all the sweeter as several of our dear friends from the West Coast, England, and Germany were at ringside. Some of the other handlers with lesser awards pushed their way in front of Ziir and me for their win photographs. I did not care. Californians, East Coasters, Finns, English, and New Zealanders celebrated that night in an Italian restaurant, and bites were saved for tired Salukis.

The flight back was uneventful and I never was hassled because of my traveling tool kit.

Ziir's ribbons are still bright on our trophy shelf and when I close my eyes, I can feel the prickly sweat running down my back and taste the thirst-quenching beer from those four days in the Lexington sun. But what my friends and family remember and chide me about, is that the best male Saluki at the National Specialty was the dog that I didn't want to take in the first place.

Brian Patrick Duggan is writing a book on the early 20th-century English adventurers who acquired Salukis in the Middle East. He has been published internationally and his historical article on Lawrence of Arabia and Salukis won the coveted Maxwell Riddle award of the Dog Writer's Association of America. Brian and his wife, Wendy, successfully raise and show Salukis. He is the Instructional Technology Consultant at the California State University, Stanislaus, and an undoubted cynophilist.

✳

The air is so hot you strain to breathe. The dry grass crunches under your feet. You press the paper cup of tepid syrupy orange drink to your forehead, trying to cool your aching head. Waiting.

When it happens, the reaction is always the same. The adrenaline starts to flow, the excitement begins in the pit of your stomach and rolls upward until your mouth is filled with cotton. Your movements are automatic. You reach down, tighten the lead, give one final brush to an already spotless fur coat, and begin moving toward the most heart-searing, most competitive few moments in any sport man has devised for himself. Everything else is forgotten in those moments when you and your dog tell the judges and the world around you, "This is my best."

A thousand times you do it, and yet it never changes. The joy of victory, the hurt of losing—and still the anticipation is the same every time you walk through a ring gate and the judge raises his hand and says, "Take them around, please."

You just know that today you are going to win the BLUE.

—Eileen Schroeder, *Going to the Dogs*

Turkish Delight, Turkish Strength

*Two different cultures join in celebrating
and sharing one spectacular dog.*

DAVID, BABUR, AND I HAD BEEN DRIVING ACROSS THE DRY Anatolian plateau of central Turkey for nearly two days. We were weary, hot, and dusty. Our rented Renault wagon was falling apart, piece by piece. We figured we'd have to return to Ankara soon or there would be no doors or windows left on the car. It must have been patched up after a bad wreck and made to appear intact when we rented it in the city. The rough country roads of Turkey had shaken it apart and now dust was leaking in from all the seams and coating our sweaty bodies. Still, we were optimistic that we would find a perfect puppy in the next village. So we kept driving.

My husband, David, and I had flown to Turkey from eastern Canada in search of Akbash dogs. These large white dogs could only be found in certain regions of Turkey where they had been guarding sheep, goats, and their masters' possessions for centuries. We were impressed with this hardy breed, the excellent working temperament, and how they adapted to North American conditions. We had in fact begun to breed them ourselves. This was our

147

second trip to find new dogs for our breeding program back home. It was no way to spend a vacation.

Neither of us spoke Turkish, except for a few words such as thank you, hello, white sheep dog, puppy, goodbye. We found an interpreter at the Ankara Veterinary Faculty, a young student surgeon named Babur Bilir, who spoke reasonably good English. He was given permission to accompany us on our quest, for which we were most grateful. For Babur, a trip into the countryside was also an adventure. He was a city kid. We learned, too late, that he was unfamiliar with some of the customs in the Muslim culture. For instance, David, being an affable, congenial person, shook hands with and waved hello to everyone he met. One time he waved at a wagonload of women returning from field work. A local Turk who was showing us a place where he knew of some dogs, exploded in the back seat and yelled at Babur, gesticulating wildly. We watched Babur's deeply tanned face turning dark red.

"What's he saying, Babur?" I asked him, while he seemed to be apologizing to the angry man.

"He says David must not look at the women or acknowledge them in any way. It is not proper for any man to look upon a Muslim woman, unless he is married to her." I thought about all those women David had shaken hands with and what must have happened afterwards. They probably had to wash their hands. From now on I watched my friendly husband like a hawk, and slapped his wrist anytime it popped up in an automatic wave. The Turks must have thought us very strange, indeed.

We did learn other, more enjoyable customs in our search for Akbash dogs. As we drove into each village, we stopped our car whenever we saw a group of people sitting at a tea house. Turks love to drink tea, usually in small, clear glasses, no milk, lots of sugar. *"Chai"* they call it. When they saw us approach, a Western man with greying hair and beard, a Western woman with short dark hair and long pants, and our Turkish interpreter in jeans and a loose tunic, they invited us to join them for tea. We would sit with them, sometimes outside on a verandah, sometimes inside, at small tables. Babur would begin to chat with them, telling them who we were and what we were doing touring so far from all the popular tourist sites.

After a while, he would tell us it was time to show the photographs. We handed over several photos of our Akbash dogs from back home, so there was no mistaking what we were looking for. They would pass the photos

Akbash is a Turkish word meaning white head. Karabash *means black head and is another type of dog used in Turkey for livestock protection.*

—CH

around, from hand to hand, pointing at them, talking, nodding their heads. More time would pass, more tea would be poured and consumed. Babur would begin to press them for information, if they had such dogs anywhere in the vicinity. More discussion followed. Sometimes they would shake their heads and tell us there were none around, but try this other particular village. Other times they said that yes, they had seen some around. Babur would ask where and who had these dogs.

If we were lucky, they would tell us exactly where to find these pure white dogs.

Occasionally, they would go to their homes and bring a dog to show us. We were often disappointed. They brought small dogs, brown dogs, spotted dogs, yellow dogs but not Akbash dogs. The dogs we were looking for are large, weighing 80 to well over 100 pounds, always white with black noses, lips, and eye rims, and brown eyes.

On this last day of our search, we drove past a small mosque and noticed a group of men sitting outside and drinking tea. We had never seen this particular combination, but decided to stop and speak with them. It was a good decision.

As usual, we were invited to drink tea with them. After the formalities and passing round of photos and discussion, one young boy ran home and brought a large, yellowed bitch who had been nursing pups. We admired her, measured her height and videotaped her. Then another man left and returned with a white dog, a little smaller, but a nice representative of the breed. We commented on how we liked this dog. Then, as if a signal had been

given, the square filled with people and dogs. We were kept busy
measuring and photographing for the next half hour. Every now
and then David would stop the camera, rewind, and show them
what we had just filmed through the eyepiece.

Finally a young man named Yaman brought his prize puppy, a
male about three months old. Immediately David and I knew we
were looking at an extraordinary pup. He was perfect in every way,
except that his joints seemed a little swollen. They explained to us
that this pup had been selected to replace their oldest dog, and he
had been fed nothing but milk so he would grow strong and large.
In fact, an all-milk diet does the opposite and was likely the cause
of the swelling.

We told Babur that we really wanted to buy this pup and to do
his best to convince the owner. So began a long process of per-
suasion and resistance. Yaman was as adamant. He would not part
with his puppy for any amount of money. This pup was too special. Babur was equally determined. His arms were up in the air, he
seemed to be shouting. We asked our enthusiastic interpreter to
please not cause such a fuss or insult the man. If he refused to part
with the pup, so be it. We were truly disappointed. We had been
unable to convince a shepherd the previous day to sell us the most
beautiful bitch we had ever seen. She resembled our favorite female back at home, with long, flowing white hair, a graceful long
body and the agility of a running gazelle.

Babur persisted in spite of our instructions. The other men
made a large circle around the pair, like you might see at a boxing
match. We began to worry that we might end up in serious trouble if he became too aggressive. All of a sudden, he turned to us
and said, "He has agreed to give you the puppy. But he does not
want money. He wants to present you with the puppy as a gift to
take back to Canada. I told him it was necessary that you have this
puppy. These are the best dogs in Turkey and the world. It would
be a great honor to send this fine pup to Canada, so he can make
more puppies for you. Isn't that so?"

Yes, we nodded our heads with delight and disbelief. Yaman was
also smiling and he and David shook hands. As a woman, I stayed

in the background, trying to contain myself. We wanted to give Yaman something in exchange for the pup and asked Babur to find out what he might like.

Babur spoke to him further then turned to us. "He won't say. But you need to buy him something, to give him a gift in return. It is expected." We then arranged to return the following day to exchange gifts. I was still not completely sure the pup was ours, but we headed back to the largest town in the area to find a suitable gift.

After settling into the hotel, we gave Babur some money and sent him shopping. He returned in an hour with a large boom box and smaller radio. He had also ordered a huge box of pastries and candies to give to the village children.

The next day we drove back to the village, to the home farm of Yaman. When we entered the farmyard we noticed fresh blood on the ground just outside the house. The men of the house greeted us and invited us inside. They asked us to sit around a low table. As we settled ourselves in the carpet-covered floor, we asked Babur what was happening.

"They will serve us a meal," he explained. "The blood we saw outside was from a freshly slaughtered lamb. This meal was prepared especially for you." David and I were most impressed. The men began bringing bowls and platters of wonderful Turkish specialties. Lamb kebob, rice, steamed vegetables, and even sweet colostrum, the first milk from a ewe that has just lambed. There was also *ayran*, a soured milk something like yogurt, and sugary hot tea, of course. As the men's smoke filled the room, I excused myself and went outdoors. They actually seemed relieved to see me go. We had already presented Yaman with our gifts, and Babur told us he and the village elders were pleased with them. Once outside, I noticed the women in their traditional head covers and long wool dresses hovering around an adjoining building. I smiled at them and they came forward, smiling shyly.

The women spoke to me, apparently excited. I did not understand what they were saying, so I thanked them in my limited Turkish vocabulary for the wonderful meal they had prepared. My attempt at communication resulted in more energetic, unintelligible chatter. I regretted that I did not have any smaller gifts to give them. They seemed happy just to be standing next to me on such an important occasion.

We finally left the village, the pup in the car with us, the owner proudly waving goodbye. David did not look at the women. We hobbled back to the rental agency in our rattling car, having collected a total of four dogs on that particular trip, two adults and two pups. Crates had to be built for the dogs since none were available at the airline we were flying with. The complications of passing through customs inspection at the airport, even with all the required documentation, was a nightmare. Eventually we did board our plane, the dogs were loaded into the cargo hold, and we began a 36-hour odyssey back home.

Yaman's pup did grow into our expectations of him. He was strong, large, handsome, and protective of his sheep yet friendly to people. We named him after his owner and later discovered the word means strength in Turkish. Yaman made a significant contribution to our North American gene pool of Akbash dogs by producing many beautiful pups for us. He died at the age of five after a bout of bone cancer. Even through horrendous pain Yaman remained strong and stoic to the last day of his life. To all who knew him, he was a true delight.

Orysia Dawydiak has been traveling with dogs for seventeen years and writing about them for nearly as long. In 1991, she and her husband, David Sims, won a Dog Writers' Association of America award for their book Livestock Protection Dogs—Selection, Care, and Training. *She has just finished a children's novel whose main characters include a number of humans and, you guessed it, dogs!*

★

One of the great moments in having a male breeder for Canine Companions for Independence (CCI) was receiving a phone call requesting the services of our dog, Dudley Do Right (aka Willy). A big, gorgeous golden retriever, he was known around the CCI vet clinic as Old Reliable: always ready, willing, and able to fulfill his duties. It never occurred to me that any male breeder would be otherwise, but what did I know? I was merely Willy's chauffeur and the CCI vet clinic was Willy's destination of choice. We both loved those special trips to CCI more than any other journey. After the car had passed our usual haunts, Willy would catch my eye and stand up in the back seat. And when I turned left onto a certain street way on the other side of town, his tail would start slapping the rear windows and he would wink at me. By the time I pulled into the CCI parking lot he was jumping the car seats, licking my face between barks, and fogging up the rear windows.

At the vet clinic, his leash firmly grasped in both hands, I would follow my lurching Casanova to his favorite spot on earth: The Breeding Room. Here the 50 commands he had mastered to become a CCI breeder would become a dim memory and he would sit ready, willing, and panting heavily, with an eager, wolfish grin on his face.

Dudley did indeed Do Right by CCI. Over the years his devotion to and zest for his "duty" yielded more than 100 CCI puppies.

Willy is now retired as a breeder, but he still loves to break up the boredom with a car trip. And he still woofs and whines whenever we approach CCI—hope springing eternal in his golden heart.

—Christine Hunsicker, "The Breeding Rounds"

KENT AND DONNA DANNEN

Could Karibou Reach Caribou Pass?

The canine companions of wilderness hikers
open new vistas.

KARIBOU, NICKNAMED BOO, WAS THE FIRST DOG TO WIN THE Samoyed Club of America's highest working award. He had led many Samoyed sled teams, had earned SCA's annual award for Top Samoyed Sled Dog, and had won the Sled Dog Class at various Samoyed specialty dog shows. He had also carried packs equaling 25 percent of his weight to many high passes and summits in Colorado's Indian Peaks Wilderness. But he had never hiked the 11,851-foot tundra meadows and cliff-hugging trail of Caribou Pass.

A dozen years earlier, the grandeur of Caribou Pass had impressed us so much that we had named our prized puppy for the place. Details, responsibilities, and coincidences of life had kept us from climbing back to the pass with its namesake who made countless other wilderness excursions much easier and much more rewarding.

Boo had turned twelve in early fall and was slowing down. Injury and kidney disease had conspired with time to make him an old dog, but they had not made him content to relax in non-working retirement. His chief delight still was to enrich his owners' wilderness experiences. Our hopes turned again to the pass we had not visited for many years. Could we lead Boo to his namesake place? Was he still fit enough to make the climb?

Neither we, nor Boo, nor two younger Samoyed pack dogs Glacier Lily and Maroon Belle, could hike far beyond the wilderness boundary when an early snowstorm frustrated our first attempt. As we loaded the dogs into our minivan, a coyote trotted across the trailhead parking lot, barely visible in the blowing snow and fog. All three dogs and the coyote seemed to share satisfaction and contentment with retreating before the storm. They were all at peace in recognizing when to quit, more at peace than we humans were, and we learned from their acceptance.

John Muir, we remembered, had shared a stormy experience with his dog Stickeen in the Alaskan wilderness of Glacier Bay National Park and gained significant insights from his canine companion. Muir wrote of the dog, "through him as through a window I have ever since been looking with deeper sympathy into all my fellow mortals." This sympathy made Muir the most famous advocate for conservation of wilderness, wilderness that converted dogs into windows to the otherwise invisible viewpoint of wild animals.

When we started up the path to Caribou Pass a few days later, the wild animals were active as they emerged from suppression by the autumn snow. Boo often alerted us to things he had smelled or heard along the trail. We noted a yellow-rumped warbler, now dressed in its drab fall feathers, about to head south. Farther up the trail, a pika scurried among the rocks, eager to complete the harvest of flowers that would be winter food.

Mostly, though, we guessed about the canine translation of what Aldo Leopold, a founder of the Wilderness Society and of the profession of wildlife management, called "olfactory poems that who-knows-what silent creatures have written in the…night." He once wrote, "My dog…persists in tutoring me with the calm patience of a professor of logic, in the art of drawing deductions from an educated nose. I delight in seeing him deduce a conclusion, in

the form of a point, from data that are obvious to him, but specu-
lative to my unaided eye. Perhaps he hopes his dull pupil will one
day learn to smell."

Most modern adherents to Leopold's land ethic who wonder at
the wisdom revealed in his classic *Sand County Almanac* do not take
seriously his self-description as a "dull pupil." Years after the climb
to Caribou Pass, however, we heard from Nina Leopold Bradley
that her father meant what he wrote. He could gain so much wisdom from the wilds, she said, because his modesty let him learn
from his dogs.

If Leopold's German shorthaired pointer was a professor of
logic, Karibou was a professor of geography. Bred by Arctic
nomads to pull sleds, carry packs, and herd reindeer over long
distances, Karibou's breed was not inclined to stationary pointing.
Our Samoyeds preferred to pull their owners up the trail and over
the ridge.

> *The Samoyed, naturally a jolly animal, puts himself into the sled game as readily as he does any other. More than anything else he wants to be part of the action whatever the cost in exertion or even danger to himself.*
>
> —Roger Caras, *The Roger Caras Dog Book: A Complete Guide to Every AKC Breed*

Secured by leashes to our
waists, the dogs practically lifted
us up the steep trail, making our
journey seem easier and shorter
than when we had hiked it without a sled dog boost. Our packs
were lighter as well, for the dogs
hauled some of the necessary
gear in their packs, leaving room
in ours for guidebooks, binocu-
lars, and cameras to better un-
derstand and enjoy the riches offered by Indian Peaks.

It was an advantage obvious to hikers we encountered at the
abandoned Fourth of July Mine. They laughingly asked to buy our
dogs on the spot but had to be content with just photographing
them.

The rusted bits of mining machinery near tree line turned our
thoughts to those who had preceded us in the wilds by as much as
11,000 years, people whose motives and attitudes toward the
wilderness were necessarily different from ours. We were the first

wilderness travelers who did not view these mountains as human habitat from which a living had to be wrenched. Earning a living here was hard; and death for a variety of reasons was not surprising. Those of us who saw Indian Peaks as a recreational resource, however, got our food from supermarkets and expected protection from high-tech gear and rangers.

If the ghost of a Paleolithic mammoth hunter had hidden in the dwarf willows and watched two groups of modern hikers at Fourth of July Mine, our technology and motives would have been as strange as though we had descended from the stars. The hiding ghost, however, would have joined in admiration of Karibou, Glacier, and Rooney, and would have recognized the leashes and dog packs as his own tools.

The dogs were tremendously important for us because they were our only link to the past, a link that was necessary to give us a sense of belonging in the wilds. Without this reference point, many other wilderness values would have faded.

Our friends of the moment passed from the mine down the trail, and we resumed hiking toward Caribou Pass, pulled upward by our dogs. High on the tundra near the rock-rimmed tarn, Lake Dorothy, we met a young woman hiking alone with her yellow Labrador retriever. The dog wore no pack, and his red leash was not attached to his owner's waist. She also was traveling pretty light, with a small pack and the long-legged, lithe build of a runner.

Perhaps her dog supplied the sense of security desired by many women and some men who prefer to hike alone. Because people who hike alone presumably prefer to be alone, we did no more than greet the young woman and her lab in passing. We did not really know if her dog was along for security or just for fun.

In the company of dogs, a hiker can have the benefits of solitude from other people without the natural discomfort of solitude. Dogs are pack animals and can provide us humans with the pack's sense of well-being and security without compromising the benefits of wilderness solitude.

Moreover, dogs can enhance the sense of solitude that sometimes is hard to come by in any wilderness area with unavoidably high visitation. Most of these visitors come from an urban environment where they have learned, with justification, to be wary of strangers. Such wariness usually is of slight value in the wilds, but good urban habits are hard to leave behind at the trailhead. More by their companionship than by their real defensive value, dogs can help hikers reduce their fear of other wilderness visitors who are present but probably not dangerous.

Sometimes, however, the danger may be real. Donna and a female friend were hiking in the Never Summer Range on the west edge of Rocky Mountain National Park. Denied canine companions by national park rules, they had to leave Karibou home.

They missed him greatly when some presumably drunken men saw them from cliffs above and decided it was clever or alluring to yell obscenities and roll down boulders on the women. Donna and her friend evaded the rocks easily as they retreated down the valley. What they could not evade was extreme mental discomfort as they camped that night. Karibou, who looked like a small, white wolf despite his friendly disposition, would have restored much of the peace that men had stolen from those women.

But on this trip Karibou was with us, and he answered easily our question about his fitness to climb to Caribou Pass. We, however, did not lead him there. He led us and answered in many ways many other questions that we had not known to ask. Just for the fun of it, he led us a half mile farther for a different view of Caribou Lake far below and across its deep valley to glacier-carved, snow-dusted Apache and Navajo peaks. Karibou led us to his namesake pass, making the trip easy, fun, informative, and inspirational. We should not have been surprised; he had performed these services for us throughout his long canine life. He would do so again.

Kent and Donna Dannen are award-winning writers and photographers who live with their son Pat in Boulder County, Colorado, near Indian Peaks Wilderness. Exactly one year after Karibou's death, they received notice that this story would be published in Travelers' Tales: A Dog's World, *an up-lifting coincidence. It is not Boo but another of their wonderful Samoyeds that graces the cover of this book in a photograph taken by the Dannens in the Rocky Mountains.*

✳

My dogs become my ears and my nose, and often my eyes. Always on guard duty, at night I feel like I can relax more than I used to when I hiked without dogs. Their incredible sense of smell and awareness often alerts us to danger or often times other birds or animals of which we may not have been aware. When we learn to pool our abilities, the making of a team and not master and dog gives us a greater sense of sharing the wilderness for our mutual benefit.

—Gary Hoffman, *Hiking With Your Dog*

JUDITH BABCOCK WYLIE

Dog Biscuit Diplomacy

How to win friends and influence pooches.

OUR SMALL GROUP WAS SITTING IN A VAN IN THE PARKING LOT OF the Benbow Inn, in Northern California, waiting for our driver, each of us content in that drugged reverie that a huge breakfast of cured ham, biscuits, and grits can produce. Suddenly, something hit the side of the van. We looked out to see a mangy brown dog snarling and snapping, his quarry the Dodge van. He backed off a few feet, barking, holding the vehicle at bay. We noticed our driver in the distance, descending the steps of the inn, gauging the gauntlet and wondering if he'd make it.

Reaching in my purse, I pulled out a large dog biscuit, and sailed it out the window as far beyond the animal as I could manage. The dog grabbed the biscuit and retreated under a bush. Fellow passengers burst into applause, and the driver boarded the van.

This was my first effort at diplomacy by dog biscuit. I had no idea then that Milkbones would become an indispensable item on future packing lists. If our beloved mutt Moxie had ever made it through obedience school, I wouldn't have a wardrobe in which every pocket bulges with a suspicious bone-shaped lump. Useful for luring her back into the house after a walk, or distracting her from lunging at another dog, I found dog biscuits were much more convenient to carry than her favorite food: whole avocados. An assortment worked best: small for daily bribes, extra-large for long car trips.

The following year I was visiting a health retreat on Hilton Head Island in South Carolina. The fitness instructor led us on our first walk, past a lush golf course with many water hazards and lagoons. Parked on one green were two suspiciously shaped logs.

"Alligators," said our pert leader. "Keep your distance. They like to sun themselves on the greens, and they're pretty harmless if you don't get too close. But take care; they're faster than they look."

Every day as part of the spa regimen, we were expected to walk two miles after every meal, either with others or alone. After lunch on the second day I set out by myself on a path that wound past the golf course. Sure enough, one of the lumpish creatures lay out in the sun, eyes shut tight. I slowed down. Even though he was on the other side of the green, near the flag, his snout was pointing in my direction.

I felt in the pocket of my warm-ups. Aha, a biscuit. Medium. I tossed it long and low, aiming beyond the beast. It fell short, coming to rest on *my* side of the alligator. The animal did not move, but one eye opened very slowly, like a recalcitrant patio door being opened. I walked on quickly. When I came back down the path fifteen minutes later, the alligator was in the same position, but the biscuit was gone. I tried not to think of the worst scenario: that perhaps a small dog had come along, bit into the biscuit, then in turn had been grabbed by the 'gator. I preferred to dwell on the best-case image; that the biscuit just offered the beast a little dietary variety to frogs and fish.

A few months later on a day trip from Monaco I was strolling the morning farmer's market in Nice, on the French Riviera, and was drawn to a table at the back of the square where a man wearing a soft cap was selling olives. Standing near the man, by the table, was a big blonde dog, whose jaunty facial expression mirrored that of his owner. Great photo, I was thinking, as I reached down for my camera. The dog quickly ducked under the table.

"*Il ne veut pas le photo,*" his owner said and shrugged.

Slowly I reached in my camera bag and pulled out a green biscuit. "*Est ce que il veut avoit un gateau de chien?*" My French is marginal, but "dog cake" seemed close enough. The man shrugged again and handed it to his dog. The animal took the biscuit carefully, placed it on the ground and studied it, thoughtful as any Frenchman of what he was about to eat. He took a bite and I got the photo.

Perhaps the dog biscuit's finest travel moment occurred in Toronto, when it was not a diversion, but an item of personal security. Friends and I were taking the bus back to our hotel, close to midnight, when the driver dropped us at a corner three blocks from our hotel, saying it was as close as his route came to it.

We began to walk down a dark street towards the hotel when one of us, a savvy New Yorker, urgently whispered, "Stop! Turn your rings around and walk back the other way." I looked behind us. Sure enough, three large rough men were bearing down on us. A shiver of fear took me by surprise. I unconsciously stuck my hands in my pockets, where I felt an extra large dog biscuit. I wrapped my hand around it and thrust it aggressively forward, hoping it looked like I was packing a gun.

I ignored the credibility problem—the chances of a middle-

While dog biscuits might be a fine snack for someone else's dog, many of us feel that our fur family deserve the best and that often means human food.

The healthiest people foods for your dog are raw vegetables (except onions), and dogs are usually fond of carrots and green beans in particular. With a minimum of calories and fat, vegetables deliver lots of vitamins and fiber.

The following foods can be toxic to dogs and, in sufficient quantity, possibly fatal: Chocolate—*the caffeine and other compounds can affect a dog's heart and central nervous system;* onions *and* garlic *contain large amounts of sulfur which can cause blood problems;* moldy foods*, including cheese, can trigger muscle spasms or seizures;* salty foods *can also be a problem for many dogs and it's best to avoid them.*

—CH

class, middle-aged woman wearing a London Fog raincoat would be slinging a gun are pretty remote. Nevertheless, during those endless moments of prickly fear, I actually felt some solace, gripping my mealy "piece." Finally the thugs passed us, although staring aggressively the whole time. Never mind. It worked for me. Now when friends ask for advice on what to do about personal security when traveling, I have an answer. Don't pack a gun. Pack a dog biscuit.

Having said that, I still have to say as food they have their limitations. The only animal you can't feed them to is yourself. More than once I've felt a little hungry on a long trip, only to look in my purse and find plenty of dog biscuits, but nothing for me. I've often gazed at them longingly, wishing they were Oreos.

Judith Babcock Wylie lives on an organic farm in Santa Cruz, California, with her husband Frank and her dog Moxie. A small grove of avocado trees grows near the fence just outside her cabin office. All were planted by Moxie, who never met an avocado she didn't either eat or bury to eat later. Judith is the editor of Travelers' Tales: Love and Romance.

✳

The mobile home I used during a brief stay in Tijuana, Mexico, sat on a neighborhood street of modest homes with fenced yards and flowering brushes. The first time I went to a café for breakfast I was met by the fierce barking of a very angry brown dog. He was fenced in and made no attempt to reach me, but exercised his fright factor on anyone coming near his gate. An older curly-haired black dog hung back, watching.

"Brownie" greeted me thus several times that week. He would hide behind a bush or tree until I was directly in front of the gate and then lunge at me with explosive barking. The object of the game seemed to be a startled reaction and quick exit by intruders, but this was getting old. Even crossing the street to avoid the heart-stopping attack did not deter this domain protector.

I devised a plan to end his bullying once and for all with a water pistol squirting vinegar-water, just to show him who was boss. Then I softened with the recalled image of a stray dog I had seen a few days earlier: a pitiable sight with its ribs jutting out and tail tucked under. Brownie was well-fed, but in the name of all *pobres perros de Mejico* I tossed some cookies to the "terror of Tijuana." He was so busy snapping them up I went by without even a snarl. Ah, Success!

I spent the next several days across the border setting up a new office in Chula Vista, a San Diego suburb. When I returned to my early morning coffee routine in Tijuana and walked by Brownie's house I heard no menacing threat or even a single bark. Half-way up the block I felt something wet in my hand. Brownie had put his muzzle right in my hand for more cookies, but his canine buddy still kept his distance. Such a turnaround called for another ration of cookies.

Brownie never barked at anyone again. After that, even if I had no cookies I was met with respectful silence. We had become friends.

—Bill Case, "The Terror of Tijuana"

ALISON DAROSA

Dogging It in Canada

A wish is granted: sled queen
for a day.

WE'RE OFF! ICE CRYSTALS, KICKED UP BY 32 POWERFUL PAWS, sparkled in the sun, stinging my face. I was at ground level, cocooned in down, snuggled into the bed of a long, wooden toboggan bouncing along the frozen midsection of Spray Lake in the Kananaskis Country of Alberta, Canada. The only sound was the *sssshhhh* of the sled's runners across the frozen lake—and occasional orders barked by the young guide at the steering bow of the sled. I lay back, resuscitated my citified lungs with the pristine blue-sky breath of the Canadian Rockies and wallowed in the awesome natural beauty that edged in around me along the Continental Divide. It was a perfect moment.

But hey, what I really wanted was a chance in the driver's position. Since childhood afternoons watching Sergeant Preston roam the Yukon in black and white, I'd envisioned myself leading a team of huskies through a frozen, white wilderness.

My opportunity came soon enough. Amanda Sinclair, the manager of the sled dog tour, asked me to take command of the team while she searched for the trail that had been obliterated by newfallen snow.

My job was to stay put with the dog team until she called for us. I stood on the foot brake. Both feet. All my weight. The emergency brake was a grappling hook I'd nonchalantly planted in the fresh snow. No sweat; I was in control.

With the agility of a deer, Amanda took off in an easy jog through powder that reached mid-thigh. I watched—and so did the dogs—as she loped up the bank of the lake.

Then, in a split second, the dogs lurched into action. Their burst of energy flipped me off the foot brake, flat-backward into three feet of powder. I scrambled upright in time to see the driverless sled disappear behind a snowdrift, dragging a useless grappling hook as if it were a tattered wedding-car decoration.

"Whoa!" I shouted. "WHOA, WHOA, STOP, NO, COME BACK!" It was like talking to a teenager.

The dogs' excited yips segued into a celebratory group yowl. I don't know what Sergeant Preston would have done; I laughed at myself. And I yelled for Amanda.

She headed the dogs off at a ridge, then boarded the bounding sleigh Indiana Jones style. She eventually stopped the team; then they all waited as I slogged through the deep snow—twenty minutes of full floundering—to reach them. By that time, I wasn't laughing; I was wheezing.

Over the rest of that day and the next one, I almost got the hang of it. On day two, I even managed to get the toboggan airborne a couple of times, on purpose and without falling off, as the dogs raced over a roller-coaster wilderness trail reserved only for that particular dog sledding outfit's use. It was wonderful fun: chills, spills, and thrills amid awesome beauty and good company. The experience was even better than I'd anticipated.

My overnight dog sledding adventure had begun at 8:30 a.m.—before the crack of dawn in this part of Canada during February. Amanda had fetched me at the inn where I'd spent the night; she ferried me to the kennels.

The minute we pulled up in her ratty, old Ford pickup (276,195 kilometers, or more than 171,000 miles on the odometer), the dogs knew what it meant. All 60 broke into song. Each had its own tune but the pitch was a common one: Choose me, choose me. These dogs are bred to run; it's what they live for.

I and the other two adventurers on this trip, an English couple named Paul and Anne, helped Amanda feed and water the dogs. They shared 50 pounds of chicken, 35 pounds of cooked rice, and 35 pounds of dog food, all sloshed together with plenty of water laced with maldoxitrin, a carbo-loaded cocktail.

The dogs were smaller and leaner than I'd expected.

"They're athletes," Amanda said. How many plump athletes do you know? These jocks, she told me, are capable of running 100 miles a day while hauling 300 pounds or more.

We helped load the chosen few into individual kennels in a transport truck. At Spray Lake, about twenty minutes away, we helped harness them, eight huskies to each of two sleds.

By this time the dog sledding tour owners, Connie and Charley Arsenault, joined Amanda and the three of them instructed the three of us in the rules of dog sledding.

The term "mush" went out of fashion with Sergeant Preston and "B" movies. "We say 'hike,'" Amanda said. "Say 'gee' (pronounced like the letter G) to go right. 'Haw' is left. 'Whoa' means stop."

"Don't ever go faster than you feel comfortable going," Charley said. "Start controlling your speed at the top of a hill. It takes about twenty yards to stop. If you tip your sleigh over, just hang on."

"No matter what happens out there," Connie added, "never, never let go of your sled."

Right. Amanda and I teamed up on one sleigh. Paul and Anne, both first-timers in their 30s, got the other. It was a morning of ups and downs.

I broke the "never-never" rule numerous times. It was that or have my arms pulled out of their sockets.

Lunch was a welcomed break. We collected dead spruce branches for a small pit fire. We saved the straightest, strongest branches to spear and roast Bavarian, cheese-filled, smoked sausages. We wrapped the sausages in buns; each of us ate at least two. For dessert, we shared carrot cake and bannock—an unleavened Native-American-style bread Connie had baked fresh that morning. We spiked the bread on our spruce spits to warm it, then drizzled it with maple syrup. We drank steaming hot chocolate.

Back on the trail again, we spent the afternoon laughing at ourselves and at each other. We gaped at the scenery. And we got to know our dogs.

> *I often wonder what the dogs think about during the day. They look forward to the noon break, because they get to sleep. Toward the end of the day when the sleds up front stop or turn to the side, or if one of the skiers stops or bends over to take off his skis, the dogs go into a sprint, because they know it's quitting time.*
>
> —Will Steger and Jon Bowermaster, *Crossing Antarctica*

Flo, a two-year-old Alaskan husky, was the youngest of my team, and as rambunctious as any two-year-old. Audi, at age ten, was the oldest, the gentleman in the crowd, a born leader who rode shotgun and kept the wild woman to his left in tow. That was Madonna, the surprisingly shy black leader of the pack.

Samson, with killer-blue eyes, was a malamute with long hair and a black-and-white mask. Maggie Mae, an overweight Siberian husky with short, stocky legs, was along for the ride more than the work. She loved it when we stopped; it was her cue that it was time to play. But it was Schooner, a lovable blond husky with sad, sleepy eyes, who stole my heart; I wanted to take her home. She was so much like the dog I loved as a child.

"I'd never sell any of these guys," Connie told me later. But she understood when I fought back tears.

The dogs loved playing; we played with them every time we stopped. But they were happiest when they were running at open throttle, heads down, hard at work, powerful and oblivious to the befuddled mushers who drove them. When we stopped, they rolled in the snow to cool off, like children rolling in the surf at the beach in August. Sometimes they took quick naps.

As the sun dipped behind Mount Fortune, the snow reflected the soft lavender of dusk. But soon the sky turned sullen, and a few fat snowflakes drifted lazily to Earth. It was our cue to high-tail to

Westside Camp, a Provincial campground on the northwest shore of Spray Lake, where we spent the night.

I'm not sure whether it was the smell of bacon cooking in a cast-iron skillet that awakened me or the sound of the sizzle. It was 9 a.m.—about twenty minutes after daybreak.

Light flurries continued to fall outside as Charley cooked eggs to order atop the woodstove inside the teepee. He piled our plates with thick slabs of Canadian bacon and more fresh-baked bannock that his wife had brought in that morning. (Connie had spent the night at home with their two small children.)

"It's cold outside," Connie said, encouraging us to help ourselves to seconds. "You're burning off lots of calories just keeping warm. Plus the whole time you're driving the sled, you're flexing muscles you've never used before. I start my season at 140 pounds. When the season's over, I weigh 115 and have to use suspenders."

That morning, we had a few options. We could go snowshoeing, ice fishing, build an igloo or do more dog sledding. All of us wanted to get back on the trail, to cut fresh tracks in the carpet of snow that had fallen overnight.

This time I rode with Charley. We headed north on a trail which bumps and curves through the wilderness adjacent to Banff National Park. The Arsenaults lease the land from the Alberta government and have exclusive use of it.

"Keep all your weight on your legs," Charley said as we took off, sharing the steering bow, one of us on each runner of the sled. "The handlebar is just to catch if you start to loose balance on the corners. You just lean back in and pull yourself up again. Keep your knees slightly bent. Put your weight on the runner in the direction you're turning."

We sped along, exhilarated. Airborne over moguls. When we got into trouble, Charley made a show of regaining control of the sled. Even the time it tipped over. He held on, dragging precariously one-handed, until he was back in control.

Eventually he opted to ride up front in the bed of the toboggan and left me in charge, alone, at the steering bow.

He knew what was coming.

"It's not so bad," Charley shouted, as I got my first look at the
steep hill we were about to descend. From up front, he couldn't see
the look of doubt in my eyes. "We're going down to the bottom,
where we're going to make a 180-degree turn. It's just that the second part of the 180-degree turn is back up a little bit of the hill."

A narrow river, only partially frozen, flowed a few feet from the
elbow of that turn.

"Good, good," Charley shouted as we headed down. "When we
get there, you'll be braking with your left foot and have your
weight on your right and really be leaning out. Don't be afraid."

"Good. Now. You're doing great. Really exaggerate your lean.
Squat down, grab out, really lean. Move into it. Great. Great.
Congratulations! You did..."

I couldn't hear what else Charley had to say, only the faint
sound of more gab fading into the distance.

I was face down in the snowbank at the bend of that turn, wondering how long it would take Charley to realize his sled had no
driver.

Alison DaRosa is travel editor of the San Diego Union-Tribune, *where
this story first appeared.*

✳

We keep between seven and ten big dogs. The cost for dry food in commercial 50-pound bags is a little more than a thousand dollars a year.
Additional expenses include harnesses and line, wormer and vaccination
shots. All of it comes to about a fourth the cost of a standard snowma-
chine.

A machine, of course, requires gas and oil and spare parts and a pair of
special tubular snowshoes to strap on the back of the seat for the inevitable breakdown way the hell out somewhere without the proper tools
to make repairs.

We bring in all our supplies with the dogs—windows for the new
bedroom addition and firewood. We travel to the mountains with the

dogs. They're not as fast as a new machine, but the time spent coming and going is serene. It's impossible to hear the forest above an engine's scream.

The dogs reveal much about the landscape we travel through: new routes, concealed wildlife, hidden crevasses, the joy of being out in the silence of the woods, which they feel, too. Machines are faster. So what?

—Richard Leo, *Way Out There: Modern Life in Ice-Age Alaska*

Locum

Sometimes the old ways of healing are best.

DOING LOCUMS IS A FASCINATING WAY OF SEEING HOW THE OTHER man lives. There are an infinite number of ways of running a small animal practice and Stewie Brannan's was one of the more bizarre ones. It was a strange quirk of fate that one of the most traumatic and demanding cases I can remember should crop up in Stewie's surgery where drugs and equipment were frighteningly minimal....

A locum (from the Latin locum tenens) is a temporary substitute, especially for a doctor or clergy member. It is used more often in England than the U.S. and means literally, (one) holding the place.

—CH

I held the curtains apart as [a well-dressed couple] staggered in and placed [their] burden on the table.

I could see the typical signs of a road accident; the dirt driven savagely into the glossy gold of the coat, the multiple abrasions. But that mangled leg wasn't typical. I had never seen anything like it before.

I dragged my eyes round to the girl. "How did it happen?"

"Oh, just in a flash." The tears welled in her eyes. "We are on a caravanning holiday. We had no intention of staying in Hensfield"—(I could understand that)—"but we stopped for a newspaper, Kim jumped out of the car, and that was it."

I looked at the big [golden retriever] stretched motionless on the table. I reached out a hand and gently ran my fingers over the noble outlines of the head.

"Poor old lad," I murmured and for an instant the beautiful hazel eyes turned to me and the tail thumped briefly against the wood.

"Where have you come from?" I asked.

"Surrey," the young man replied. He looked rather like the prosperous young stockbroker that the name conjured up.

I rubbed my chin. "I see...." A way of escape shone for a moment in the tunnel. "Perhaps if I patch him up you could get him back to your own vet there."

He looked at his wife for a moment then back at me. "And what would they do there? Amputate his leg?"

I was silent. If an animal in this condition arrived in one of those high-powered southern practices with plenty of skilled assistance and full surgical equipment, that's what they probably would do. It would be the only sensible thing.

The girl broke in on my thoughts. "Anyway, if it's at all possible to save his leg something has to be done right now. Isn't that so?" She gazed at me appealingly.

"Yes," I said huskily. "That's right." I began to examine the dog. The abrasions on the skin were trivial. He was shocked, but his mucous membranes were pink enough to suggest that there was no internal haemorrhage. He had escaped serious injury except for that terrible leg.

I stared at it intently, appalled by the smooth glistening articular surfaces of the tibio-tarsal joint. There was something obscene in its exposure in a living animal. It was as though the hock had been broken open by brutal inquisitive hands.

I began a feverish search of the premises, pulling open drawers, cupboards, opening tins and boxes. My heart leaped at each little find: a jar of catgut in spirit, a packet of lint, a sprinkler tin of iodoform, and—treasure trove indeed—a bottle of barbiturate anaesthetic.

Most of all I needed antibiotics, but it was pointless looking for those because they hadn't been discovered yet. But I did hope fervently for just an ounce or two of sulphanilamide, and there I was disappointed, because Stewie's *menage* didn't stretch to that. It was when I came upon the box of plaster of Paris bandages that something seemed to click.

At that time in the late '30s the Spanish Civil War was vivid in people's minds. In the chaos of the later stages there had been no proper medicaments to treat the terrible wounds. They had often been encased in plaster and left, in the grim phrase, to "stew in their own juice." Sometimes the results were surprisingly good.

I grabbed the bandages. I knew what I was going to do. Gripped by a fierce determination, I inserted the needle into the radial vein and slowly injected the anaesthetic. Kim blinked, yawned lazily and went to sleep. I quickly laid out my meagre armoury, then began to shift the dog into a better position. But I had forgotten about the table, and as I lifted the hind quarters the whole thing gave way and the dog slithered helplessly towards the floor.

"Catch him!" At my frantic shout the man grabbed the inert form, then I reinserted the slots in their holes and got the wooden surface back on the level.

"Put your leg under there," I gasped, then turned to the girl. "And would you please do the same at the other end. This table mustn't fall over once I get started."

Silently they complied and as I looked at them, each with a leg jammed against the underside, I felt a deep sense of shame. What sort of place did they think this was? But for a long time after I forgot everything. First I put the joint back in place, slipping the ridges of the tibial-tarsal trochlea into the grooves at the distal end of the tibia as I had done so often in the anatomy lab at college. And I noticed with a flicker of hope that some of the ligaments were still intact and, most important, that a few good blood vessels still ran down to the lower part of the limb.

I never said a word as I cleaned and disinfected the area, puffed iodoform into every crevice and began to stitch. I stitched interminably, pulling together shattered tendons, torn joint capsule and fascia. It was a warm morning and as the sun beat on the surgery window the sweat broke out on my forehead. By the time I had sutured the skin a little river was flowing down my nose and dripping from the tip. Next, more iodoform, then the lint, and finally two of the plaster bandages, making a firm cast above the hock down over the foot.

I straightened up and faced the young couple. They had never moved from their uncomfortable postures as they held the table upright, but I gazed at them as though seeing them for the first time.

I mopped my brow and drew a long breath. "Well, that's it. I'd be inclined to leave it as it is for a week, then wherever you are let a vet have a look at it."

They were silent for a moment, then the girl spoke. "I would rather you saw it yourself." Her husband nodded agreement.

"Really?" I was amazed. I had thought they would never want to see me, my smelly waiting room or my collapsible table again.

"Yes, of course we would," the man said. "You have taken such pains over him. Whatever happens we are deeply grateful to you, Mr. Brannan."

"Oh, I'm not Mr. Brannan, he's on holiday. I'm his locum, my name is Herriot."

He held out his hand. "Well thank you again, Mr. Herriot. I am Peter Gillard and this is my wife, Marjorie."

We shook hands and he took the dog in his arms and went out to the car.

For the next few days I couldn't keep Kim's leg out of my mind. At times I felt I was crazy trying to salvage a limb that was joined to the dog only by a strip of skin. I had never met anything re-

motely like it before, and in unoccupied moments that hock joint
with all its imponderables would float across my vision.

There were plenty of these moments because Stewie's was a
restful practice. Apart from the three daily surgeries there was little activity, and in particular the uncomfortable pre-breakfast call
so common in Darrowby was unknown here.

Little things enliven the week, but the tension still mounted as
I awaited the return of Kim. And even when the seventh day came
round I was still in suspense because the Gillards did not appear at
the morning surgery. When they failed to show up at the afternoon session I began to conclude that they had had the good sense
to return south to a more sophisticated establishment. But at 5:30
they were there.

I knew even before I pulled the curtains apart. The smell of
doom was everywhere, filling the premises, and when I went
through the curtains it hit me: the sickening stink of putrefaction.

Gangrene. It was the fear which had haunted me all week and
now it was realised.

There were about half a dozen other people in the waiting
room, all keeping as far away as possible from the young couple,
who looked up at me with strained smiles. Kim tried to rise when
he saw me, but I had eyes only for the dangling useless hind limb
where my once stone-hard plaster hung in sodden folds.

Of course it had to happen that the Gillards were last in and I
was forced to see all the other animals first. I examined them and
prescribed treatment in a stupor of misery and shame. What had I
done to that beautiful dog out there? I had been crazy to try that
experiment. A gangrenous leg meant that even amputation might
be too late to save his life. Death from septicaemia was likely now
and what the hell could I do for him in this ramshackle surgery?

When at last it was their turn, the Gillards came in with Kim
limping between them, and it was an extra stab to realise afresh
what a handsome animal he was. I bent over the great golden
head and for a moment the friendly eyes looked into mine and
the tail waved.

"Right," I said to Peter Gillard, putting my arms under the chest. "You take the back end and we'll lift him up."

As we hoisted the heavy dog on to the table the flimsy structure disintegrated immediately, but this time the young people were ready for it and thrust their legs under the struts like a well-trained team till the surface was level again.

With Kim stretched on his side I fingered the bandage. It usually took time and patience with a special saw to remove a plaster, but this was just a stinking pulp. My hand shook as I cut the bandage lengthways with scissors and removed it.

I had steeled myself against the sight of the cold dead limb with its green flesh, but though there was pus and serous fluid everywhere the exposed flesh was a surprising, healthy pink. I took the foot in my hand and my heart gave a great bound. It was warm and so was the leg, right up to the hock. There was no gangrene.

Feeling suddenly weak I leaned against the table. "I'm sorry about the terrible smell. All the pus and discharge have been decomposing under the bandage for a week, but despite the mess it's not as bad as I feared."

"Do you...do you think you can save his leg?" Marjorie Gillard's voice trembled.

"I don't know. I honestly don't know. So much has to happen. But I'd say it was a case of so far so good."

I cleaned the area thoroughly with spirit, gave a dusting of iodoform, and applied fresh lint and two more plaster bandages.

"You'll feel a lot more comfortable now, Kim," I said, and the big dog flapped his tail against the wood at the sound of his name.

I turned to his owners. "I want him to have another week in plaster, so what would you like to do?"

"Oh, we'll stay around Hensfield," Peter Gillard replied. "We've found a place for our caravan by the river—It's not too bad."

"Very well, till next Saturday, then." I watched Kim hobble out holding his new white cast high, and as I went back into the house relief flowed over me in a warm wave.

How lucky I was that in those days the Spanish Civil War was still fresh in my memory. I would never have dared to encase Kim's leg in plaster if I had not read of the miraculous recoveries of the soldiers whose terrible wounds had no other means of treatment.

After more than 30 years of veterinary practice in Yorkshire, James Herriot decided to write about his experiences in what he thought would be his only book, All Creatures Great and Small. *In that book, the first of many best-sellers, Herriot described his career goals; he always wanted to be a veterinarian and was sure he would become a small animal surgeon "treating people's pets in my own animal hospital where everything would be not just modern but revolutionary."*

★

We have our vet to thank for getting us on the road with our dog. After our beloved shepherd-lab, Arthur, had his clocked cleaned by the neighborhood chow who had taken out a Doberman the month before, we rushed him to the vet's office and sat, nervously awaiting the outcome. We were in a quandry: the next day we both *had* to leave for a business trip to Las Vegas—something we couldn't get out of. But could we leave Arthur with his usual babysitter, a dog-loving, but twelve-year-old, girl?

One look at Arthur when the vet brought him out to us—weak-kneed and wobbly—gave us our answer. "He's not as bad off as he looks," said the vet, which should have been reassuring except that half of Arthur's face was swollen to twice its normal size and his shaven scalp was a ripe shade of purple. "He's going to need round-the-clock antibiotics and bandage changing, though." We knew then that Arthur was about to embark on his first trip to Las Vegas.

After a ten-hour drive—and a phone call to make sure that our hotel would accept dogs—the three of us limped into the lobby of the Holiday Inn located on the Vegas Strip. The manager of the front desk watched our approach with a smile that slowly dissolved into a grimace as we closed in on his counter. He darted to his computer and started tapping away in a frenzy. By the time we reached "Registration" he was ready for us. He handed us our room key, holding it with the outstretched tips of his fingers as though it were contaminated. It was only after we had checked into our room that we realized that not only didn't we have neighbors in the adjoining rooms, but we were given an entire three-story wing of the hotel, one that had been locked tight for remodeling.

That evening we took a walk down the Strip to work the travel kinks out of our legs. The night air was balmy and the stainless-steel stitches holding Arthur's face together twinkled, reflecting the gaudy neon casino lights. Tourists approaching us stopped mid-laugh, averted their eyes, and leapt off the sidewalk as they became aware of Arthur on a leash heading towards them. We felt like Moses parting the Red Sea.

—Brian Erwin and Christine Hunsicker,
"Have Dog, Will Travel"

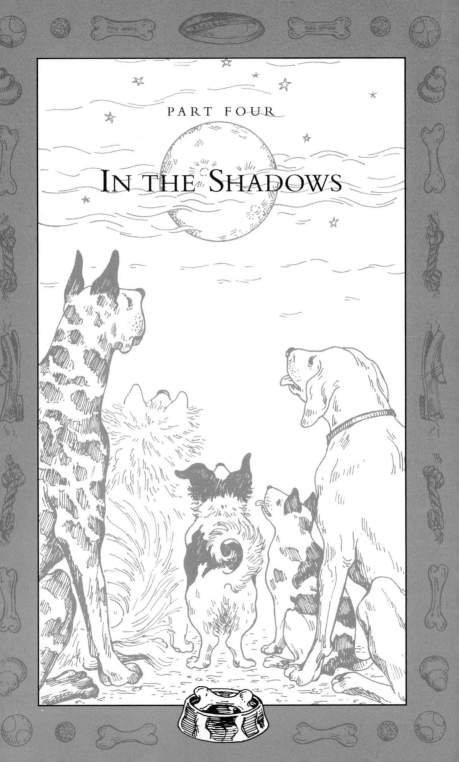

PART FOUR

IN THE SHADOWS

Rabies!

Every dog lover's nightmare.

RABIES. THE WORD MAKES ME SHUDDER. IT IS THE ONE THING I
continually feared in India. And not without cause. I was told
many times by my Indian friends of the fearful pain of the rabies
shots they endured as children when they were bitten by an animal feared rabid. Fourteen shots right in the stomach. My own
stomach contracts in fright just thinking about it. But you can't
take chances; if the animal isn't caught, can't be found, or, god for-
bid, proves rabid, you have to have the shots or you will die. And
die a horrifying death; I don't even want to think about the nature
of such a death.

Thirty years ago my husband, Harry, a psychologist, signed a
contract with a USAID (United States Agency for International
Development) team to work for two years in New Delhi, India.
For all of us, Harry, myself, our three pre-teenage children, Linda,
Eddie, and Jimmy, it was a wildly exciting adventure. We had not
traveled outside the North American continent much less lived in
a country half-way around the world in a culture very different
from our own. We were naïve, novices, babes in the woods who
had much to learn, some of it the hard way. Particularly about
dogs.

183

In India then (it is less true today) pye—wild—dogs roamed the streets, even in the capital city of New Delhi. They belonged to no one and scavenged for food wherever they could find it. They were lean, cunning, fierce creatures with a predatory look in their eyes. I feared them.

If you are bitten by a suspected rabid animal, first wash the wound immediately with lots of soap and water. Immediately notify a doctor or the Department of Health and ask for help. A substance called rabies immune globulin (RIG) can be given to neutralize the virus at the site of the wound. The RIG is then followed by a series of rabies vaccine shots (usually 5 shots), given over 28 days.

—Hawaiian Government Health Website:(www.hawaii.gov/health)

But not Linda, Eddie, and Jimmy. They thought all dogs were pets; they had no basis for knowing otherwise. Even Harry was having a hard time changing his attitude. He was a chronic sympathizer with the outcast and rejected; he personalized his relations with them, treating them as he would like to be treated in their place. He often found it difficult to treat an animal as an animal with its own rights and needs. I thought his sympathy—warm-hearted, but wrong-headed—sometimes inappropriate and potentially harmful. In the case of Bhuli I thought his concern downright dangerous. We fought over that dog for many months, which upset the children.

I suppose Bhuli could have been called a handsome dog—lean, short-haired, with a long, intelligent face. She was a creature of the streets who was friend of the jackals and, unfortunately, of our children. She quickly learned that we were a dependable source of food and showed up at our compound daily. The children petted her and played with her as long as she would allow them to before loping off to join her pack. I tried to run her off every time I saw her but without much luck. She would sidle away, then return as soon as I wasn't around. Our gates were always open—we weren't used to living behind walls. I couldn't get Harry to agree to shut the dog out. He was as bad as the children about feeding her; he wouldn't take my worries seriously. But Jaggu, the cook and Om Prakash, the sweeper, did. They were as worried as I was. "Bhuli," they told us meant "crazy," which I'm sure they thought we were. They were alarmed and resentful that we foreigners had such poor judgment as to befriend a pye dog like that one. I agreed with them.

One day a few months after Bhuli had become a member of our extended household, Linda came home from school breathless and wide-eyed. That morning a puppy had run on to the grounds of the American International School which she and Jimmy attended and bit six children and a teacher. All seven had to endure the painful anti-rabies shots. The puppy was rabid. And we all knew that only a week before a governess attached to the embassy of another Western nation had died of rabies despite having had the shots.

Bhuli never saw the inside of our compound again, and even Harry and the children agreed with that decision. There was no pleasure in such a vindication, just the realization that we had been unquestionably lucky.

Betty Ann Webster is a clinical social worker, a freelance writer, an oral historian, and a committed (compulsive?) traveler. Thirty years ago she lived and worked in India for two years. She has returned there eight times and intends to continue returning whenever possible.

✴

When my husband was sent to Ireland to set up a floppy disk plant, we thought long and hard about how to cover all bases. Everything was fine except for one thing: our dog Bentley. Ireland required a six-month quarantine for all pets entering the country.

My husband asked all his Irish contacts if there were "exceptions" and they all said, "No." When we read that Liz Taylor was ensconced in a boat outside of London because she wouldn't submit her dogs to the quarantine, we knew that Bentley would have to face the inevitable.

The kennel was expensive but that doesn't ensure total success. Our first visit to the kennel, just outside of Dublin, was reassuring. Each dog had its own immaculate six-foot bunker and was walked regularly. However, there was no interaction between the dogs because of the rabies threat.

We later learned that, during the first week when Bentley refused to eat, the kennel owners cooked him fresh meat which he couldn't resist. One time when we visited him—like a relative in jail—we met the teenage girl who walked him every day, and watched Bentley nudging up to her. This was all very reassuring.

Finally, the six months were up and Bentley came home and lived with us in Ireland for five years. I have to say that as nice as his quarantine experience seemed to us, his stay in the kennel had changed his personality. Forever after he was more timid and fearful than the pet we had known. On the other hand, in Ireland's entire history, there has never been a single case of rabies.

—Audry L. Lynch, "The Case of the Quarantined Dog"

Visions of Puppies Danced in My Head

*A dog lover comes to terms with
the puppy markets of Asia.*

I NEVER MUCH BELIEVED IN THE BIOLOGICAL CLOCK THING—THAT
inevitable rush to propagate and then spend the rest of your life
taking care of something small and cuddly. But in Asia, something
happened; I was a walking sack of maternal yearnings, wanting to
care, to feed, to pet all things small and furry. I needed a puppy.

It first hit me while I was walking through the animal market
in Yogyakarta on Java. Tucked behind the birds and rattlesnakes,
the hanging bats and boxes of locusts, was a corner just for puppies. The iron cages were stacked one atop the other, with puppies of varying colors and sizes, some healthy-looking, but most
scraggly and diseased. I had been told and had long ago prepared
myself for the sight of "man's best friend" caged and ready to sell
to the first hungry buyer. These dogs were not for the dog-lover
or mother in one; these puppies were not for pets, but rather a delicacy in Indonesian cuisine. The tender morsels apparently "melt
in your mouth," said an American expatriate I met later that
evening. "And you can tell if it's not a puppy," she had said seriously, almost accusingly. "Tough. Very tough."

A week later in northern Thailand, I told the hotel manager,

whom I had recently befriended, about my growing maternal ob-
session. "Have you seen the puppies under the kitchen?" she asked
casually, understanding my dilemma. My face lit up. My internal
caretaker started shifting into gear.

"Puppies?!" I gasped. "Where?"

I spent the rest of the evening sitting on the ground next to a
slight rise where the kitchen floor met the cold, dirt ground. With
some difficulty I dragged a small puppy from hiding, then, with
one emerged, the other three were quick to follow. The dogs were
slices of heaven; soft black and white balls of love and energy just
waiting for me to care for them.

I took my job seriously. Every day after sightseeing, I would return to my "kids" and offer them a bowl of milk. We would play
and frolic until nightfall, or until my traveling companion, Julie,
invariably dragged me from the scene and lectured me about not
getting attached to Asian dogs. "Don't fall in love today with what
you might eat tomorrow," she warned me. But it was too late. And,
anyway, the hotel staff assured me these puppies were destined to
be pets, not dinner.

It had occurred to me that my attachment was growing unnat-
ural, even perfect strangers were telling me so. But nothing could
prepare me for the shock of returning from a three-day trek in the
jungles of Thailand to find my babies gone. "Stolen," said the girl
at the hotel. "Probably for money." I walked the streets depressed
and downcast, a mother who had lost her children.

Each day I stopped by the Western supermarket outside of
which was a woman with an iron cage full of puppies for sale. I
checked to make sure none of them was "mine," then sat down and
proceeded to play with them as long as the vendors (or the dogs)
could tolerate. I fluffed them up, trying to make them shiny and
pet-like, unlike the street dogs that had mange and appeared mis-
treated. These scavengers walked with their heads bowed low and
their tails between their legs. Any movement in their direction
generally sent them fleeing in terror.

Julie worried about me. Then she became frustrated and we

started arguing in public. Cultural norms are different here, Julie would say sternly. "Dogs are not the same domesticated children they are in the West. In Asia, dogs are considered dirty, filthy animals."

It helped me to imagine a foreign tourist in America sitting in a pen of pigs with her arms around her favorite swine. I would have to react with an equal dose of confusion and disgust, the same that I garnered in Asia. All the same, I couldn't be stopped from caressing a dog each time I saw one; or searching out the animal market each time we were in a new city; and I would always search the menus for dog meat.

> "The domestic dog," zoologist James Serpell observes, "has become the Western equivalent of the sacred cow. Dogs are cherished and nurtured as man's best friend, and the idea of killing and eating one is virtually unthinkable. Yet, throughout much of the New East dogs are reviled as symbols of all that is filthy and degraded, while in China, Korea, and the Philippines they are cooked and devoured with enthusiasm."
>
> —Marjorie Garber, *Dog Love*

In Laos, the dogs seemed less afraid, which made sense to me, considering the Lao people were gentler and calmer all around. I didn't see dog meat on the menu but at the night market, right next to my favorite crepe stand, was a woman who for two weeks straight had a bowl full of charred puppies on her table. At first, I wasn't even sure they were dogs—their little bodies were rodent-like, with their tail and teeth still fully attached—so I asked a local boy to confirm my suspicion.

"Not many people can afford such good meat," he told me. He also put to rest my fear (and that of many travelers) that I might be slipped a slab of dog unknowingly. "The meat is too expensive," he explained. "You would have to order it for it to be served to you." But by this time I had grown far more comfortable with the Asian diet. In fact, I was not only open to the idea of such different foods, but started to search out some of the more bizarre offerings: fried frog skin in Thailand, snakewine in Vietnam, and buffalo blood soup in Laos. I had even developed a hint of carnivorous curiosity about dog meat, though I would never say it out loud nor would I ever act upon it.

By my third month of travel, it was obvious that my constant craving was calmed a bit, my irrational behavior toned down. Though I still yearned to take a puppy home with me, to pet a stray dog, or to visit the animals in the local markets, my thoughts felt more reasoned and more culturally sensitive. Thinking back to one of my first weeks in Indonesia, I had certainly come a long way.

My transformation had begun during one of my final visits to the animal market in Java when I was still at the height of my irrational desperation to show the puppies of the world a bit of care and love. I began the day as a kind of mad activist with misdirected maternal instincts, but by sundown had begun to realize the futility of my quest and the enormity of the life of the dog in Asia.

I was completing one of my daily oblations at an animal market in the center of Yogya. I came upon cage after cage of puppies soon to be on someone's dinner plate and in their soup pot. At first I simply pried my fingers in through the metal grate and caressed the small spots of silken fur. The heaving masses of warm puppy flesh were deep in slumber, trying to escape the dreaded equatorial heat. They looked peaceful, completely unaware of their culinary appeal. But they did look hot. Too hot. And it was up to me to cool them down. I wasn't about to open the cage doors á là PETA and yell for the animals to "Run, free yourselves!" Instead, I took my water bottle with the spray top from my backpack and created a small pool in the corner of the cage. They didn't notice. Then, with a single squeeze, I managed to cover three sleeping pups with a gush of water. Suddenly, everything was in motion.

All the pups awoke and lunged toward the water, lapping furiously at the small dark spot. They were dying of thirst! I started trying to aim the water into their mouths then thrusting my wetted fingers through the grate. They started yelping and clawing at the cage walls. The stall keeper slowly peered around the corner to see what the commotion was. He had the look of disgust and slight amusement I had grown accustomed to. I smiled weakly, becoming more and more traumatized by the frenzied puppy mass. They yelped and clawed, tumbling over one another in a desperate attempt at a drop of water. My drop of water. Had I not offered, they never would have known how thirsty they actually were. Their yelps began to arouse the animals in the neighboring cages. At my feet, a cage full of kittens started to mew loudly and I knew I had to flee.

I clumsily stuffed my water bottle back into my pack and ran toward the crowded exit of the market. Past the screeching parrots, the chickens, the cats, and so, so many dogs, I stumbled onto the street, ashamed, knowing I had failed in my attempt to somehow save or appease the puppies of Asia. To appease my own maternal instinct and the absurd notion that caring for a puppy or two could change the miserable lives of dogs everywhere, I had been overwhelmed by the intensity of what I assumed to be the dogs' need as well as at their poor treatment. But there was nothing I could do.

Leaning against the wall outside the marketplace, my breath still heavy and hands shaking, it finally started to dawn on me: there is never enough you can do—never enough money or food or love to give to all the needy children and animals of the world. My backpack was still hanging, half-open, and the water bottle was on the ground at my feet. I leaned over, picked up the bottle and took a long drink of water. This is motherhood, I thought to myself. Better get used to it.

Zélie Pollon is a San Francisco writer and editor. She recently left her job as Managing Editor of Curve Magazine *to travel the world teaching, writing, and playing with dogs.*

✦

One evening in the small Filipino port city of Olongopo, my friends invited me out to dinner for a special occasion. I knew where we were going. Half of me was in disbelief and denial. The other half in giddy excitement, as though we were children sneaking into a neighbor's orchard to steal apples. We walked for many minutes—my friends led me "this way, now this way," to a hidden bend in the wicked city's guts. Colored lights at the end of a short alley announced the place.

We walked in and sat down and, without warning, the gravity of the step I was about to take stole upon me and dulled the ardor of my adventurous palate. I was about to eat man's best friend, true companion of my own childhood. It suddenly seemed like cannibalism. I began to think of excuses. Maybe I could say I wasn't hungry. Yeah. Or that I had a touch of the Asian flu. Sure. But it was too late to repent now. The die was cast when the waitress set the dish in front of me. My hosts were looking at me with expectation in their eyes, and the words "We trusted you" hanging on their lips, ready to be spoken. Outside, in the back of the restaurant, a dog yipped as it met the knife.

With grim determination I thrust my spoon into the chunks of meat, splintered bone, and pieces of vegetable. I sampled the broth; my guts churned. A thousand huskies howled. I chewed fourteen times and swallowed, defiantly. I looked up to see my hosts smiling broadly with relief.

I would be no honest man if I did not tell you that it was tasty. The flavor was somewhere between beef and pork, and it was very tender. It was, after all, a puppy. The broth was seasoned with garlic and vinegar and the vegetables were fresh and not overdone. My hosts sucked the bones with satisfaction, but I didn't join them in that. Afterwards, I bade them goodnight and thanked them for a truly pleasant evening. Then, to quiet the little howls and whimpers echoing in my stomach, I went out and got drunk.

—Richard Sterling, "A Dog Tale"

KELLEY L. HARRISON

Missing Chanel

The loss of a beloved pet in a
strange town brings kindness,
generosity, and even hope.

SOMETIMES IT HAPPENS. LIFE GRABS US BY THE THROAT AND shakes us around. Often there is no answer to the question, "Why?" One wouldn't think that losing a pet could cause such turmoil, but I have now packed that unenviable experience into the luggage of my life.

Chanel weighed only two pounds, a feisty little Yorkie who feigned ferociousness with her bark but portrayed timidity in her character. Strangers frightened her and my arms were her safety net. She was smaller than the squirrels she liked to chase, and playing with dogs held no interest to her. She seemed to think horses were somehow her kin.

Chanel liked to cuddle and lick and snuggle close. Nestled in my purse, she accompanied me to the bank, the store, the movies, once even to the theater, where she sat on my knee and watched the goings-on with the rest of the audience. On our walks, after she'd tire out, I'd tote her in front of me, propped up in a newborn baby carrier. Others passing by did double-takes, and had to stop to coo over the hairiest infant they'd ever seen.

She came into my life at a time when I needed unconditional love. Personal and professional difficulties had confused and depressed me, and Chanel provided a delightful diversion. Not long after she arrived, I took an unspecified leave of absence from my husband and my work. I packed my bags and my pooch into the car, and drove across the country searching for answers to questions I couldn't articulate.

Chanel bounced around with me for thousands of miles, for almost a year. We shared faded motel rooms and hours of driving along dusty back roads, encountering new faces and avoiding old problems. Each day brought its own challenge, but the unknown seemed an adventure, not a fear. Chanel carried on like a miniature trooper in the face of it all. She kept me in the moment, her Yoda-like expression always asking, "What's next, what's next?"

I worked odd jobs along the way, usually on farms, where people didn't ask many questions but opened their doors to both of us. Though my wallet stayed slim, they fattened Chanel on table scraps and allowed us to bunk together. We didn't care about much more.

We ended up in Louisville, working on a horse farm. Up at daybreak, I mucked and fed and rode. Chanel followed or roamed nearby, keeping an eye on my every move. The end of each day found both of us spent and dirty, but loving it. We had been there only two months when it happened.

Searching for a dog her size is not easy. She had escaped from a friend's house during our dinner out, and four of us looked for her that night for hours. We wandered through neighbors' yards and peered under bushes and in drainage ditches, the glows of our flashlights searching for two tiny red eyes in the darkness. I called for her until I was hoarse. I didn't believe she would go far. I thought she was afraid and hiding, and by morning she would show up.

She didn't. And for the next two weeks my life came to a standstill. Nothing mattered to me except finding Chanel. I contacted Animal Control, the Humane Society, animal rescue organizations. I called vets' offices and the newspaper, offering a large reward for her return. Hoping that Chanel might find them, I scattered her food and my clothes in different locations, only to later discover them untouched.

My husband and sister joined me for several days and we passed out 1,200 flyers and put up posters. Local businesses and schools posted flyers in their windows. A local radio station took pity on me and disregarding company policy, regularly announced Chanel's disappearance.

Telephone calls came in, with possible sightings, and the search area expanded. I drove and walked and called for her for miles and hours. If someone had her, no one was talking.

A private investigator heard a radio announcement and donated his time and expertise for a day. He thought she might be trying to make her way back to the farm, sixteen miles from where I lost her. He plotted a possible route she might follow. Could Chanel make an incredible dog journey herself? I willed her to come back to me. Chanel, I thought, if I can't find you, you have to find me.

Sleep offered little respite, though I became physically and emotionally exhausted. I tortured myself with thoughts that I was inside and warm, whereas Chanel could still be out there—hungry, frightened, cold. A few nights it rained, and I stared out the window into the blackness beyond, my eyes and heart burning from sorrow. I prayed and pleaded, willing to barter, to be a better person, anything to keep her safe. At times it all seemed so surreal. Each passing day I spiraled downward, deep and heavy, into the thickness of a bad dream.

*D*ogs can find their way home from long distances, over terrain with which they are not familiar. This is a quality they share with cats and many other species of animals. It seems to be based on an appreciation of subtle differences and changes in the earth's magnetic field. Experimentally the ability can be impaired by the presence of powerful magnets, so that we know this is not a fantasy.

—Desmond Morris, *Dogwatching*

The kindness of strangers continued and encouraged me. Different individuals with tracking dogs volunteered their services.

Not knowing me from Adam, each spent a day with me scouring locations. Their efforts, however, proved fruitless, as the area was too urban for the dogs to pick up her scent and stay with it. Refusing payment, they offered hugs of solace and good luck.

The investigator had recommended a local psychic and I had contacted her early in the search. At the time my case seemed not a high priority to her (which intellectually I understood, but not emotionally). On the eleventh day following Chanel's disappearance, she called me late that evening. Her charting suggested that Chanel could still be in a five-mile radius from the location of her disappearance, but in very poor condition. I needed to find her soon.

Armed with heavy coveralls and a thermos of hot coffee, I immediately drove out again and searched in the cold and wind, from 10:30 p.m. until 4:00 a.m. It seemed hopeless, and physically impossible. How could I find her on foot? How could I uncover every tiny possible hiding space? What if I found her and she was dead? Finally, I lay in the dirt and waited—for a glimpse of the morning sun—for the feel of Chanel's tongue on my nose—for a chance to hold her again.

Two days later, desperate, I called another psychic, an "interspecies communicator." She lived out of state and asked only a few questions. Relaying her account of the incident, she stated that Chanel had tried to re-enter my friend's house but smacked into the glass door.

Thinking someone had struck her, she raced off in terror. The psychic proceeded to describe a woman she felt had found Chanel the morning after she disappeared—an older woman, living alone, someone who needed Chanel in her life now. She described the woman's house and car. Skepticism sounded in my voice. Then she told me that Chanel liked to sit on a small pillow on the floor and watch this woman put her makeup on in the morning. My gut turned. That had been Chanel's pattern with me.

Further search attempts proved unsuccessful. The phone calls stopped coming. I kept the ad in the paper and the posters up for a while. No trace of Chanel was found.

Even now, almost three years later, I carry the loss with me. My heart's a little heavier, but the blessings shine a bit brighter. The generosity and compassion of strangers and friends who helped in my time of need made me believe again in the goodness of others. And if Chanel is alive and well, then her purpose may be with another. During our time together, she taught me lessons of unconditional love, forgiveness, and loyalty. The memories remind me that I am still the student, that life is a perpetual teacher, and that loving never really has to end.

Kelley L. Harrison is a farrier and freelance writer. Her previous articles and stories have been published in Florida Today, The Times Recorder, Horizons Magazine, Driftwood XIII, *and* Driftwood XV. *She lives in Florida with her husband, two horses, a pooch, and a hedgehog.*

✳

The dogs in our lives, the dogs we come to love and who (we fervently believe) love us in return, offer more than fidelity, consolation, companionship. They offer comedy, irony, wit, a wealth of anecdotes, the "shaggy dog stories" and "stupid pet tricks" that are commonplace pleasures of life. They offer, if we are wise enough or simple enough to take it, a model for what it means to give your heart with little thought of return. Both powerfully imaginary and comfortingly real, dogs act as mirrors for our own beliefs about what would constitute a truly humane society. Perhaps it is not too late for them to teach us some new tricks.

—Marjorie Garber, *Dog Love*

PART FIVE

THE LAST WORD

PICO IYER

Dogs Abroad

A dog's world: a reflection.

DOGS I USUALLY THINK OF AS FOUR-LEGGED MUSCLE RELAXANTS, wagging counterparts to Penelope, or helicopter look-alikes with floppy ears for radars. They are creatures of hearth and home—household gods with legs—and they tie us to the places we know, and mark our territory with their own. Reflecting our secret hopes back to us, they obligingly allow us to project all our affections and fears upon them.

But dogs abroad—like everything abroad—are something else: strange and exotic and charged. They stand for all the forces we cannot touch, and, as much as welcoming us in, they keep us out. They are on home ground, their presence reminds us, and we are not. And in places we can never quite penetrate, where sorcerers fill the air, dogs stand for all the divisions we cannot see: between animals and angels, between angels and their dark inversions.

When I think of Bali, for example, in a certain mood—a troubled mood or a doubting mood—I hear only the dogs howling in the dark. So much feels enchanted on that island, where sweet-smiling sylphs bring fruit to one's room, and artists walk all day to temples, that nothing unpleasant seems allowed. Babies are carried on their parents' shoulders and never touch the ground.

But at night, when darkness deepens, Bali is given over to its dogs, and a counter-world, a shadow-realm, emerges. They are scrawny things, most often, these pariah beasts, demon-eyed and screeching, and it can seem as if all the care lavished on everything else here has left not a scrap for them. And they growl like vengeful furies, angry at being shut out from the dazzle all around. They growl, they yelp, they snarl at you as you walk the unlit lanes of Ubud. And as the night fills up with *levak* witches and spooky dreams, their presence becomes as disturbing, as dissonant, as the jangled, syncopating gamelan music one hears coming from the trees. No walk through night-time fields feels safe.

And when I think of Tibet, I think of dogs, too, but in the high silence of blue-sky days. So much of that uplifting culture is behind barbed-wire now, laid waste or mocked by invading Chinese soldiers and unwanted tanks. Yet when I went to Drepung monastery, near Lhasa, and Sera, the spirit of those evacuated centers seemed to be preserved mostly by their dogs. There were thirty or forty of them in each, sitting quietly in sun-washed lanes, or serenely posted at the entrance to old prayer-halls, never barking or stirring or creating a fuss. It was as if the dogs were the custodians of a culture whose human elements had been sent away, and protectors of a calm as strong as that of their exiled leader, the Dalai Lama. When you visit "Little Lhasa" in Dharamsala, India, you see frisky Lhasa Apsos circumambulating the central temple with their wizened keepers; but when you visit Tibet, you find the mastiffs at the temple gates, changeless and unflinching.

Temple guardians come in two kinds, perhaps, fiercely yapping and serene. But travel teaches us that even our symbols of loyalty and constancy and companionship can also exist outside of us, the watchdogs of traditions we can inspect but never claim. They sit on other sides of gates we cannot see, and remind us that, abroad, we find gods we cannot make our own.

Pico Iyer was born in Oxford in 1957 and was educated at Eton, Oxford, and Harvard. He is an essayist for Time *magazine, a contributing editor at* Condé Nast Traveler, *and the author of* Video Night in Kathmandu *and* The Lady and the Monk.

TIPS AND GUIDELINES FOR TRAVELING WITH YOUR DOG

It's easy to jangle the car keys and say, "Want to go for a ride?" when inviting our four-footed family to accompany us on a car trip to the local grocery store. Inviting them on a trip across the country or around the world is quite another matter. However, with forethought and planning, you can have all the benefits of their company while decreasing the likelihood of disaster.

Here is some good advice about car and air travel compiled with the help of *Best Friends Animal Net* magazine and The Canine Web—their web site addresses follow in the section called "The Internet Unleashed."

$\mathscr{B}$EFORE YOU LEAVE

Vet Check

Few of us enjoy traveling when we are not feeling well and it's a good bet that your dog doesn't either. Take your dog to the veterinarian at least one week before you begin your trip to be sure he is healthy and all vaccinations are current. Also, it's a good idea to ask your vet about any special problems that may exist in the area you are planning to visit. Are fleas or ticks especially bad there? Are there any diseases you should know about ahead of time? When you reach your destination, look up the phone number of the local vet—even the smallest towns have at least one veterinarian—just in case you have a canine emergency.

Paperwork

Be sure to have a current health certificate, license, and proof of all vaccinations. Many places will not allow dogs entry unless you can show them proof of a current rabies inoculation. In all our years of traveling with our dogs, we've only been asked to show these documents once, but if we hadn't had them, it would have been a long drive home. Also be sure to

THE NEXT STEP

bring the telephone number of your hometown veterinarian's office in case you have to reach them while you're away.

Fido I.D.

Your dog should be wearing identification at all times. Attach her license and identification tags to a collar that fits comfortably and yet won't pull off. If you are staying in the area for a while, add a local phone number where you can be reached in case you are separated from your pooch. Pack a recent photo of your dog, too, just in case.

A Home to Roam

If your dog uses a crate, it would be a really good idea to take it along. It's much safer for him and you if he travels inside the crate during the car trip. Also it provides a touch of home while staying in an unfamiliar place during your time away. Our small dog takes great comfort in sleeping in her crate; it makes her feel safe and is the one place she can relax. We have gone camping without her crate only once—when we ran out of space. Since that anxiety-ridden and bark-filled trip, however, we all decided we would rather leave our tent at home than her crate!

Plan Ahead

There are many hotels, motels, resorts, and campgrounds that accept pets, and at the end of this section is a list of several excellent guidebooks that will help you map out your accommodations. Always call ahead to be sure the place still accepts pets. It's also advisable to make reservations whenever possible—some motels have only a limited number of rooms available to pet owners.

There are no special requirements for traveling with a dog in any of the United States, except for Hawaii which currently imposes a quarantine on all dogs entering the state. For specific information contact Hawaii's State Department of Agriculture at 808-483-7151. If you are traveling to another country, it's best to call the country's consulate nearest you well in advance for the latest health requirements and travel advisories for you and your dog.

Manners 101

Please be sure your dog has learned the basic obedience commands such as sit, stay, come, and quiet before you embark on a trip of any length. It's safer for your dog and much more pleasant for you and all those around you if your pal knows and responds to these commands and will stay quietly by your side.

PACKING LIST

We have an old backpack that we use to carry our dogs' things when we go on a trip. Some of the items, such as towels, bowls, and spare leashes, get cleaned at the end of each trip and automatically repacked for the next adventure. Some items you might want to take are:

- A leash, a crate or bedding, and a long tie-out line for letting your pet relax when there's no fenced area.
- Food and water dishes, food from home (keep your dog on the same diet as home, if possible), good drinking water, any medication, toys, grooming brushes, towels.
- Lots of plastic bags or newspapers to clean up after your pal. This part is really essential—if we do it, nobody notices, but if we don't, then everybody is unhappy.
- First aid kit. There is a wonderful book, *Dog First Aid,* by Randy Acker, DVM, that recommends very specific items, but a general first aid kit for the average traveler should be fine. Be sure to pack some hydrogen peroxide to wash out human and canine cuts and gashes.
- A "Places to Go with Your Dog" guidebook for the area you are visiting. Believe it or not, we have come across some really fun things to do that were listed in our "dog" book but not in the "people" guide. Several titles are recommended at the end of this book.
- Spray bottle. We always travel with a 4-1 mix of water and white vinegar to remove traces of any doggy accidents. But even if you don't need that (lucky you), the bottle can be filled with water to cool off your dog or used for any number of things.
- If you don't have tinted back windows, stick-on car shades are a good

idea, especially if you have a hatchback car that can really heat up in the back without being noticed up front.

𝒪N THE ROAD

Test Drive

It's best to get your dog accustomed to riding in a car at a very young age, but even older dogs can adapt. Take them on short trips (ten to fifteen minutes) to the store or to a park for a game of fetch. Make it fun and part of your usual routine. Gradually lengthen the drives so they are in the car for a few hours. Try very hard to avoid having your dog's first car adventure be a trip to the vet.

Some dogs simply do not adapt at all to car travel. If it's really important that your dog travel with you, consider asking your vet for medication. If that fails, you may just have to leave him or her at home in a safe, stress-free environment that also provides the companionship that the dog's social nature requires.

The Paws That Refreshes

Stop every two to three hours to let your dogs stretch their legs, have some water, and relieve themselves. The break will do you all good. In fact, I now find all car trips much more enjoyable when we take along our pooches. Remember to keep your pets leashed when in rest areas to avoid unwelcomed visits from other animals and the possibility of your beloved pet running away.

Chow Time

You should try to keep your dog on a regular feeding schedule where he eats only small snacks during the day and the largest meal after you've settled in at night.

Air Apparent

Except on the coldest days, dogs will want some little fresh air so it's a

good idea to drive with at least one window open a couple of inches. If the weather is hot, open all the windows a few inches to allow some cross-ventilation. However, never roll the windows completely down because your dog could jump out of the car and be injured. Also your dog should not ride with her head out the window because bugs and dirt could become lodged in her eyes and ears.

Going Solo

If you must leave your dog alone in the car, you should only leave him or her for ten to fifteen minutes and be sure you are parked in a shady spot. Leaving your pet in the car when it's hot can be very dangerous. Find suitable boarding accommodations (such as a local kennel or veterinary office) if you plan to be away from the car for any extended period of time. In her book, *The California Dog Lover's Companion,* Maria Goodavage recommends that you "never, ever, ever leave a dog in a car with the windows rolled up all the way. Even if it seems cool, the sun's heat passing through the window can kill a dog in a matter of minutes. Roll down the window enough so your dog gets air, but so that there's no danger of your dog getting out or someone breaking in. Make sure your dog has plenty of water."

FLYING WITH YOUR DOG

Personally, I am reluctant to put my dogs in the cargo section of an airplane and since one of my dogs tops 85 pounds, he is too big to ride in the cabin. So when we fly our dogs stay home with friends or an attentive pet-sitter. However, many people do fly with their pets—frequently. Canine Companions for Independence raises and trains dogs to work as a team with differently-abled people all across the United States. Each year hundreds of these special beings are crated and sent on a plane trip and there has never been a problem other than the very occasional mis-routed pup. Still this is a difficult decision for many of us to make. Here are some basic tips to insure a safe flight for your precious cargo.

Climate control

Most airlines will not allow your dog to fly if the weather is too hot or too cold at the departure, arrival, and transfer airports. When you make reservations for your dog's flight, be sure to ask about the requirements for that particular airline or the airports involved.

Go Direct

This may be more inconvenient and expensive for you, but many pets are lost during transfer from one plane to another. A direct flight will eliminate the transfer.

The Portable Pet

If possible, take your pet in the cabin with you. Many airlines allow you to carry on small pets for an extra fee. Usually one small pet per plane is the limit. However, the definition of small differs from one airline to another so you should call around and ask the size requirements and shipping fee when making reservations for you both.

Excess Canine Baggage

If your dog is too big for the cabin, he will have to fly as "excess baggage" in a portion of the cargo hold that is pressurized and temperature-controlled. Fees for this also vary from one airline to another. If possible, make sure your pet is loaded last since this increases his chances of being taken off the plane first. Also be sure that your pet is not stored near any toxic materials, such as dry ice.

Check in with the Flight Crew

When you board the plane, be sure to mention to the flight crew that your dog (and mention his name) is on board in the cargo hold. The captain can check up on the dog during the final flight check and will make sure your dog's travel compartment has good ventilation and temperature control throughout the flight. It's also perfectly all right to ask the flight crew about your dog during the flight. I'm told that the nervous parent routine (done with humor and in moderation) goes over quite well.

The Personalized Crate

Be sure that your dog's crate is labeled with your name, home address, telephone number, and a way to reach you at your destination in case you get separated from your dog. Also, be sure to put your dog's name in large letters somewhere on the crate—on top of the door is a good visible spot—because the baggage crew will often reassure nervous dogs by talking to them, using their names to calm them.

Tipping

While tipping isn't considered necessary and is often frowned upon by the airlines, it just makes sense that someone accepting a little extra money to look after the needs of your pet might be willing to do just that.

To Tranquilize or Not to Tranquilize

This is something you should discuss with your vet before your trip. Tranquilized animals can't protect themselves from injury and during a rough flight, they might get tossed around in the crate. There are also the physical side effects to consider: vomiting and choking because they could not swallow properly, or damage to their cardiovascular systems. If your dog travels calmly in the car, then tranquilization may not be necessary. If he gets agitated in the car, then you may not have any choice.

If you decide to tranquilize your dog, you should consult with the veterinarian for the proper drug and dosage. And you should do a trial run with a small amount of the drug to rule out any allergic reactions and to determine how the drug is going to affect the pet and for how long. This way, you can best time when to give the medication.

HOTELS, MOTELS, AND CAMPGROUNDS

Most of us have been tempted to just sneak our dogs into the motel, or rather, not to mention the 90-pound canine in the back seat. Over the years I've learned that most places will accept a dog—even if the management's stand on dogs is unclear—if I ask nicely and say that my wonderful, gentle dog has been house broken for a long time and barks rarely and then only to protect me. Here are a few more guidelines to follow that will keep a hotel or motel pet-friendly.

Honesty is the Best Policy

It's best to call ahead to be sure your accommodations accept dogs, but sometimes there's no time. When you register let the management know you have a dog with you. A quick pre-registration grooming session for you and your dog will aid your quest for a room at the inn. If you are pleasant and you both look tidy, chances are good that your dog will be welcomed too.

Sleeping and Feeding Arrangements

My dogs find it reassuring to have their own special areas in the motel room. I set up their crates, bedding, toys, etc. in one corner, and place water and feeding dishes on available non-carpeted areas. If your dog sleeps on the furniture at home, bring along a big towel or sheet to put down to protect the hotel's furniture from excess dirt and fur. I also pack along a bottle of water-white vinegar mix, just in case. I'm told by non "dog people" that they can always smell a dog's presence. If a spot on the carpet or furniture smells too doggy to me, I spritz it with the water-vinegar mix and wipe it dry.

No Barking Dogs

Sometimes you can be sitting on the floor next to your dog, with your hand clamped over his mouth, begging and bribing him not to bark, but he still wants to protect you from the world outside. When this happens you can hook him up to his leash and take him on a tour of the premises and hope that stops the barking. You can also do what I did on the second night of my dog Arthur's first motel experience: I introduced him to the people on either side and told them his name. Something worked because he never barked in a motel after that.

No Unattended Dogs

Never leave your dog alone in the room. The motel is a new and strange environment for her and she might bark or try to claw her way through the door.

Even when you are in the room with your dog, you might want to put out the "Do Not Disturb" sign so that housekeeping won't come in and startle the dog. If you order room service, consider asking them to place the trays outside your door.

Leash and Clean up After Your Pet

Your dog should be kept on a leash at all times. You might want to ask the staff if there is a specially designated area to exercise the canine guests or if there is a park nearby where you can run your dog off-leash. Please pick up after your dog. Too many complaints might stop the dogs welcome policy.

Consider a Kennel

If you are really and truly stuck and cannot find a place that will take your dog, or your dog just isn't "hotel friendly" get out the phone book and call around to the local kennels. Sometimes veterinarians also take in boarders. If there is a dog park in the area, ask the people there for a recommendation.

Campground Canines

Most state and national campgrounds in the U.S. require that dogs sleep in the vehicle or tent. A dog sleeping outside, tethered to a tree, is at risk for attack from the surrounding wildlife. Never leave your pet unattended or they will show you just how quickly they can become undomesticated.

DINING WITH YOUR DOG

Your dog may not be able to get a seat at your table as dogs often do in Paris, but many restaurants in the United States and Canada have outdoor dining that will accommodate you all. The dog's al fresco presence is generally at the discretion of the management so it's best to check the restaurant's pet policy before you order.

Your dog should remain under the table and out of the path of table servers and other customers. You should restrain your dog from begging from other tables and please do not bring along a dog prone to fighting. It's hard for us dog lovers to remember that there are people who do not like dogs and some people are frightened of them.

You and your dog are always acting as ambassadors for the rest of us who like to travel with our pets. If your dog (and you) behave well, chances are good that all of us will be welcome guests again.

ℋIKING AND BACKPACKING WITH YOUR DOG ——

Terri Watson, author of the excellent "Hiking/Backpacking with Canines" page on the Internet (snapple.cs.washington. edu/canine), offers the following advice.

Who can participate? You must be (1) physically able to restrain your dog(s) in the presence of distractions, such as a running deer or squirrel, and (2) responsible enough to prevent the dog from being a nuisance to other people or animals. This includes picking up after your pets.

If you choose to have your canine carry a pack, you should be confident she is in good health and structurally sound. Consider having your pet's hips X-rayed in order to check for hip dysplasia before asking her to carry a full pack over long distances.

Collar, Tags and Leash

You will need a collar with identification and a leash. Terri uses a rolled leather buckle collar onto which she attaches the rabies, dog license, and identification tags. Her leash of choice is a six-foot long, round synthetic leash, with a loop for the hand and a sturdy snap. While retractable leashes

offer the dog more freedom, they tend to get tangled in bushes and other people easily.

Booties

Depending on the type of terrain, the weight of the pack, and the dog's tendency to tear his footpads, you might wish to buy booties to protect your dog's feet. There are many types of booties, suited to different terrain.

Pack

Terri uses a two-part pack. A pad is attached to the dog with three straps: across the chest, around the body right behind the front legs, and around the body near the end of the ribcage. The pack attaches to the pad with a plastic buckle at the center front of the pad and three velcro strips; one large one down the center and two smaller ones on the sides. Don't over-tighten the straps as they can be uncomfortable for the dog and interfere with breathing and motion. Terri prefers the two part pack design because it allows her to quickly remove and replace the pack during rest stops.

Identification

Tattoos and microchips are two other forms of identification (in addition to collar tags) for your dog. Unfortunately, for these techniques to allow recovery of your pet, more knowledge on the part of the person finding the dog is required. Check with your local shelters to be certain of the procedure they follow with lost dogs.

Vaccinations

The dog should be current on all regular vaccinations. You may want to ask their vet about additional vaccinations or medical precautions applicable to the area being traveled. Some examples include heartworm medication, lyme shot, flea and tick control, and kennel cough.

Food and Water

Clean drinking water is a must for both you and your dog. Although natural water sources may be plentiful on your hike, the water may be contaminated with giardia (a protozoan parasite), or harmful bacteria or chemicals. Always make sure that you carry enough water for the hike.

Notify a Friend

You should let someone know what your travel plans are, especially when going to a less frequently traveled area.

Weather

Watch your dog for signs of heat exhaustion or stroke. Particularly, unusually rapid pant, and/or a bright red tongue or mucous membranes. Shorter-nosed breeds, such as bulldogs or pugs, may have less efficient heat exchange rates and should be watched especially closely. If you determine that your dog is overheating, you should stop immediately and get him into the shade. Terri recommends putting cool water on the dog's belly and groin area.

Trail Etiquette

Dogs are required to be on-leash on most maintained public trails. In many places the leash is required to be six feet or less in length. Just having your dog on-leash in not sufficient. You should keep him calm when passing others on the trail, preferably training him to sit quietly to one side of the trail as others walk by, or to calmly walk by others without barking or straining against the leash.

There is an etiquette to passing or being passed by horses, mountain bikers, and other hikers. Horses have right-of-way over hikers, and hikers are supposed to have right-of-way over mountain bikers. Hikers going downhill have right-of-way over those coming up. Especially with horses, try to get well clear of the trail and leave them plenty of room to pass.

Also keep in mind that not all dog owners are responsible with respect to their pet's behavior on the trail. Some will even allow aggressive dogs off-leash.

RESOURCES FOR TRAVELING
WITH YOUR PETS

ORGANIZATIONS, NEWSLETTERS, AND BOOKSTORES

In the United States, the Traveling Petowners of America (TPOA) publishes an annual (May) directory for pet travel in 48 states. For more information, write to Traveling Petowners of America, P.O. Box 6042, Omaha, NE, 68106-0042. A self-addressed, stamped envelope would be appreciated. You can also contact them via the Internet at 102005.1316@ compuserve.com.

DogGone is a terrific bi-monthly newsletter about "fun places to go and cool stuff to do with your dog." Published by Wendy Ballard, you can subscribe to it for $24 US at *DogGone,* PO Box 651155, Vero Beach, FL, 32965. The email address for DogGone is: doggonenl@alo.com.

Dog Lovers Bookshop carries a complete line of books, magazines, and other information for the dog lover. It is located at 9 West 31st Street, New York, NY 10001. Phone: 212/594-3601. Email: info@dogbooks.com. Visit their Web site at http://www.dogbooks.com.

THE INTERNET UNLEASHED

Web Sites

The World Wide Web offers some of the best, up-to-the-minute information about dogs—and some real garbage. As most dog Web sites are set up and maintained as a hobby and service by passionate dog-lovers, the information on such sites changes as quickly as their time allows. While I am recommending some sites below that I have found particularly helpful or interesting, it is by no means meant as the most comprehensive list nor is the information guaranteed to be updated regularly. Nonetheless, these sites are good starting points.

You can add to your own Internet research by participating in the dog newsgroups and by using the Web's many search engines to find Web sites that may have the content or contacts you desire. (My favorite search engines are Excite, http://www.excite.com, WebCrawler, http://www.webcrawler.com, and Yahoo!, http://www.yahoo.com.) You will be pleased by the number of dog lovers who congregate on the Internet and who are incredibly willing to share their knowledge and experience.

General Pet Web Site/Traveling with Pets
http://www.bestfriends.com
This web site is from Best Friends/AnimalNet, the electronic magazine for animal lovers. It has a great deal of useful information about traveling with pets as well as some other wonderful tidbits for animal lovers.

Traveling With Your Pet/International Import Requirements
http://vetpath1.afip.mil/Vet_Services/Dog_Center/import.req.html
Written by Major Terry Gosch, DVM, this site lists the health and legal requirements for traveling with your dog in most of the major countries. A terrific place to start your research.

The Canine Web
http://snapple.cs.washington.edu/canine
This web site offers up all sorts of interesting information about dogs and also provides many excellent links to information about traveling with dogs. Its link to hiking and backpacking with dogs is terrific.

Informational Dog-Related Web Sites
http://www.zmall.Com/pet/dog-faqs
Compiled by Cindy Tittle Moore, this is the mother-lode of dog Web sites. It features hundreds of sites organized by Canine FAQs (which stands for Frequently Asked Questions), General Canine Sites, Breed Sites (from

Afghan Hounds to Yorkshire Terriers); Rescue, Shelters, and Related Information; Newsletters, Articles, Magazines; Pet Loss Pages, Activities, and Humor.

Doggy Information on the Web
http://www.bulldog.org/dogs/
The search engine on this site lets you search its many links, including those to breed clubs, dog rescue, politics, and research.

Pro Dogs Networks
http://www.prodogs.com
Another well-built Web site that may of particular interest to breed-specific dog lovers.

Info Dog
http://www.infodog.com
Hosted by Moss Bow-Foley, manager of dog shows since the early 1900's, this site has comprehensive show information, as well as links to all sorts of other sites of interest to dog lovers.

The British Canine Shopping Centre
http://www.k9.co.uk/
A lively and active site providing a great starting point for traveling with your dog in the United Kingdom. It includes news, events, breeders, leads to UK dog magazines, and more.

Dogs Down Under
http://www.wwwins.net.au/dog/downunder.html
Almost everything you'd want to know about dogs in Australia. Includes some fascinating information about dingos and other dog breeds native to Australia.

Internet Newsgroups

Newsgroups are Internet bulletin boards organized by subject. Some have tens of subscribers and others tens of thousands. If you have a question about traveling with your dog, you can post a message to the newsgroups listed below and odds are good that one or more people will respond. Like mailing lists, newsgroups are a good way to find pen pals online who may be able to help you find what you need.

rec.pets.dogs
rec.pets.dogs.behavior
rec.pets.dogs.breeds
rec.pets.dogs.health
rec.pets.dogs.info
rec.pets.dogs.misc
rec.pets.dogs.rescue

Internet Mailing Lists

If newsgroups are like public bulletin boards, Internet mailing lists are like private clubs you join (free of charge) to share information with like-minded members. Sometimes these lists are moderated, which means there is a gatekeeper who monitors the email messages being sent from one member to the entire membership, and others are not moderated, which is more of a free-for-all. Once you join one of the mailing lists below, all of the email messages being sent among its members appear in your email box as messages; sometimes they are organized into digests, which allow you read a stream of messages instead of having to open and read each individual message.

Caninetimes ("Canine Times E-mail Newsletter")
Subscription Address: majordomo@po.databack.com
Owner: Cynthia Freyer (cfna@pullman.com)
A free email newsletter for dog owners. Features research, behavior, human-animal integration programs, service dogs, books, breaking news, trends. Published three to four times a month. In your email message (not the Subject: line) send the command "subscribe caninetimes" and your email@address to majordomo@po.databack.com.

RECOMMENDED READING

There are several excellent books for planning your globetrotting with your canine pal. If you are looking for guide that covers the area where you live, check your local bookstore.

If you are planning a trip and would like books for another region, your bookstore can order them for you or you can contact a specialty store such as the Dog Lovers Bookshop in New York.

The Dog Lover's Companion travel series published by Foghorn Press are excellent guides for traveling with your dog in California, Florida, Boston, Seattle, and Atlanta.

On the Road Again with Man's Best Friend is another excellent series with guides to the southeastern, mid-Atlantic, northwestern, and southwestern United States, as well as New England. The guides are published by Dawbert/Macmillan.

Eileen Barish, has several books on pet travel:
Vacationing with Your Pet (3rd edition) Pet-Friendly Publications. 720 pages. 23,000+ hotel, motel, inn, ranch, and bed-and-breakfast listings in the United States and Canada. *Doin' Texas with Your Pooch, Doin' Arizona,* and *Doin' New York* are also available.

Pets-R-Permitted Hotel, Motel, Kennel & Petsitter Directory. Nelson, M.E., editor. Published by Annenberg. 301 pages. 10,000+ U.S. listings. Also covers camping with pets in national parks.

The Portable Pet: How to Travel Anywhere with your Dog or Cat. By Barbara Nichols, published by Denglinger/Alpine. 80 pages. Question-and-answer format covers everything from car trips to travel around the world.

Take Your Pet Too! Fun Things to Do! written by Heather Walters, published by M.C.E. is a nice collection of fun events, attractions, and accommodations that will welcome both you and your dog.

⌐HE NEXT STEP

Two good books about hiking and backpacking with your dog are:
Hiking with Your Dog by Gary Hoffman, published by ICS.
A Guide to Backpacking with Your Dog by Charlene LaBelle, published by Alpine.

Other good resources are the books from which we've made selections and we have listed them below.

Caras, Roger. *A Celebration of Dogs*. New York: Times Books, a division of Random House, Inc., 1982.

Caras, Roger. *A Dog is Listening: The Way Some of Our Closest Friends View Us*. New York: Summit, 1992.

Caras, Roger. *The Roger Caras Dog Book: A Complete Guide to Every AKC Breed*. New York: M. Evans and Company, Inc., 1996.

Coren, Stanley. *The Intelligence of Dogs: Canine Consciousness and Capabilities*. New York: The Free Press, a division of Macmillan, Inc., 1994.

Garber, Marjorie. *Dog Love*. New York: Simon & Schuster, 1996.

Herriot, James. *James Herriot's Dog Stories*. New York: St. Martin's Press, 1986.

Hoffman, Gary. *Happy Trails for You and Your Dog: What You Really Need to Know When Taking Your Dog Hiking or Backpacking*. Riverside, California: Insight Out Publications, 1996.

Jenkins, Peter. *A Walk Across America*. New York: William Morrow & Company, Inc., 1979.

Leo, Richard. *Way Out Here: Modern Life in Ice-Age Alaska*. Seattle, Washington: Sasquatch Books, 1996.

Matthiessen, Peter. *The Snow Leopard*. New York: Penguin USA, Inc., 1987.

Mayle, Peter. *A Year in Provence*. New York: Vintage Departures, a division of Random House, Inc., 1991.

Monks of New Skete. *How To Be Your Dog's Best Friend: A Training Manual for Dog Owners*. New York: Little, Brown and Company, 1978.

Morris, Demond. *Dogwatching*. New York: Crown Publishers, Inc., a division of Random House, Inc., 1986

Mowat, Farley. *The Dog Who Wouldn't Be*. New York: Bantam Books, a division of Bantam Doubleday Dell Publishing, 1984.

Ogden, Paul. *Chelsea: The Story of a Signal Dog*. Boston, Massachusetts: Little, Brown and Company, 1992.

Paulsen, Gary. *Winterdance: The Fine Madness of Running the Iditarod*. Orlando, Florida: Harcourt Brace & Company, 1994.

Rosen, Michael J. *The Company of Dogs: Twenty-One Stories by Contemporary Masters*. New York: Doubleday, a division of Bantam Doubleday Dell Publishing, 1990.

Schroeder, Eileen. *Going to the Dogs*. New York: Crown Publishers, Inc., 1980.

Scott, Alastair. *Tracks Across Alaska: A Dog Sled Journey*. New York: The Atlantic Monthly Press, 1990.

Steger, Will and Jon Bowermaster. *Crossing Antarctica*. New York: Alfred A. Knopf, Inc., 1992.

Steinbeck, John. *Travels With Charley: In Search of America*. New York: Penguin Books, a division of Penguin USA, Inc., 1986.

Stephens, John Richard. *The Dog Lover's Literary Companion*. Rocklin, California: Prima Publishing, 1992.

Stern, Jane and Michael. *Dog Eat Dog: A Very Human Book About Dogs and Dog Shows*. New York: Scribner, 1997.

Thayer, Helen. *Polar Dream: The Heroic Saga of the First Solo Journey by a Woman and Her Dog to the Pole*. New York: Simon & Schuster, 1993.

Thomas, Elizabeth Marshal. *The Hidden Life of Dogs*. New York: Houghton Mifflin Co., 1993.

Toth, Susan Allen. *My Love Affair with England*. New York: Ballantine Books, a division of Random House, Inc., 1992.

Whittemore, Hank and Caroline Hebard. *So That Others May Live: Caroline Hebard & Her Search-and-Rescue Dogs*. New York: Bantam Doubleday Dell Publishing, 1995.

Winokur, John. *Mondo Canine*. New York: Penguin USA, Inc., 1991.

Woodhouse, Barbara. *No Bad Dogs: The Woodhouse Way*. New York: Simon & Schuster, 1982.

Index

Index of Contributors

Acknowledgements

Any book is a collaboration of talent, time, and energy provided by many people, and I am very fortunate to have had help from some of the very best.

It is no exaggeration to say that without my husband, Brian Erwin, this book would not exist. With his encouragement and support, I was able to say "yes" to this thoroughly rewarding project, and his editorial skill and thoughtful advice helped keep me on course throughout. To my extremely tolerant and delightful daughters, Shayne and Lina, I can only say thank you, and yes, I really do love you more than the dogs.

A special thank you goes to Beth Larssen and Michael Diepenbrock whose generous flexibility accommodated my erratic editing schedule into my other work life, and to Sandi Brown who provided invaluable help in finding the perfect cover photograph.

A huge thank you goes to series editors Larry Habegger and James O'Reilly for giving me the opportunity to work on this incredibly enjoyable book. Additional appreciation goes out to the Travelers' Tales team for all their behind-the-scenes support: Susan Brady, Cindy Collins, Tim O'Reilly, Wenda Brewster O'Reilly, Sean O'Reilly, Linda Noren, Leili Eghbal, Raj Khadka, Jennifer Leo, Judy Anderson, Susan Bailey, Kathryn Heflin, Barbara Garza, Nels Berthold, Jill Berlin, and Dana Furby.

I would also like to thank everyone who sent us stories about their dogs. It was a joy and an honor to read about these special canine companions and I wish we were able to publish them all.

Finally, my deepest appreciation to all the writers who have contributed to this book. Each story is a treasured piece of this canine quilt. Thank you.

"Eagle River" by Gary Paulsen excerpted from *Winterdance: The Fine Madness of Running the Iditarod*, copyright © 1994 by Gary Paulsen, reprinted by permission of Harcourt Brace & Company and Victor Gollancz Ltd.

"Sailing with Sam" by Ann Raincock published with permission from the author. Copyright © 1997 by Ann Raincock.

"Sheepdog Trials: A Field Trip" by Susan Allen Toth excerpted from *My Love Affair with England* by Susan Allen Toth. Copyright © 1992 by Susan Allen Toth. Reprinted by permission of Ballantine Books, a division of Random House, Inc.

"The Things We Do for Love" by Louise Rafkin published with permission from the author. Copyright © 1997 by Louise Rafkin.

"The Dog Who Wasn't Supposed to Go" by Brian Patrick Duggan published with permission from the author. Copyright © 1997 by Brian Patrick Duggan.

"Turkish Delight, Turkish Strength" by Orysia Dawydiak published with permission from the author. Copyright © 1997 by Orysia Dawydiak.

"Could Karibou Reach Caribou Pass?" by Kent and Donna Dannen published with permission from the authors. Copyright © 1997 by Kent and Donna Dannen.

"Dog Biscuit Diplomacy" by Judith Babcock Wylie published with permission from the author. Copyright © 1997 by Judith Babcock Wylie.

"Dogging it in Canada" by Alison DaRosa reprinted by permission from the author. Copyright © 1996 by the *San Diego Union Tribune*. Originally appeared in the *San Diego Union Tribune*.

"Locum" by James Herriot excerpted from *James Herriot's Dog Stories* by James Herriot. Reprinted by permission of St. Martin's Press and Michael Joseph. Copyright © 1986 by James Herriot.

"Rabies!" by Betty Ann Webster published with permission from the author. Copyright © 1997 by Betty Ann Webster.

"Visions of Puppies Danced in my Head" by Zélie Pollon published with permission from the author. Copyright © 1997 by Zélie Pollon.

"Missing Chanel" by Kelley L. Harrison published with permission from the author. Copyright © 1997 by Kelley L. Harrison.

Additional Credits (arranged alphabetically by title)

Selection from "Adventures in Public Access" by Terry Thistlethwaite published with permission from the author. Copyright © 1997 by Terry Thistlethwaite.

Selection from "April in the Arctic" by Barbara Ras published with permission from the author. Copyright © 1997 by Barbara Ras.

Selection from "Bali Dreams" by Larry Habegger published with permission from the author. Copyright © 1997 by Larry Habegger.

Selection from "The Breeding Rounds" by Christine Hunsicker published with permission from the author. Copyright © 1997 by Christine Hunsicker.

Selections from *Brewer's Dictionary of Phrase & Fable* (Fifteenth Edition). Copyright © 1995 by Cassell Publishers Ltd. Published by Cassell Publishers Ltd.

Selection from "Canine Culture Gap" by Shepard Barbash published with permission from the author. Copyright © 1997 by Shepard Barbash.

Selection from *Hiking with Your Dog* by Gary Hoffman reprinted by permission
of the author and ICS Books, Inc. Copyright © 1997 by Gary Hoffman.

Selection from the Hawaiian Government Health website available from
www.hawaii.gov/health.

Selection from *How To Be Your Dog's Best Friend: A Training Manual for Dog
Owners* by The Monks of New Skete published by Little, Brown and
Company. Copyright © 1978 by The Monks of New Skete.

Selections from *Hunting Mister Heartbreak* by Jonathan Raban. Copyright © 1990
by Jonathan Raban. Reprinted by permission of HarperCollins Publishers,
Inc.

Selection from *The Intelligence of Dogs: Canine Consciousness and Capabilities* by
Stanley Coren published by Macmillan, Inc., a division of Simon & Schuster.
Copyright © 1994 by Stanley Coren.

Selections from "It's Definitely a Dog's Life in France" by Judith Morgan
reprinted from the October 20, 1985 issue of the *Los Angeles Times*.
Reprinted with permission from the author. Copyright © 1985 by Judith
Morgan.

Selection from "Loose Puppy Adopts Jeff King," by Catherine Stadem reprinted
from the March 1996 issue of *Alaska*. Reprinted by permission of *Alaska*.
Copyright © 1996 by Catherine Stadem.

Selection from *Mondo Canine* by Jon Winokur. Copyright © 1991 by Jon
Winokur. Used by permission of Dutton Signet, a division of Penguin
Books USA, Inc.

Selection by Barbara Woodhouse reprinted with the permission of Simon &
Schuster and the Estate of Barbara Woodhouse from *No Bad Dogs: The
Woodhouse Way* by Barbara Woodhouse. Copyright © 1978, 1982 by Barbara
Woodhouse.

Selections from *The Roger Caras Dog Book: A Complete Guide to Every AKC
Breed* by Roger Caras. Copyright © 1980, 1992, 1996 by Roger Caras.
Reprinted by permission of the publisher, M. Evans and Company, Inc. and
Curtis Brown Ltd.

Selection from "The Ruff Guide" by Brian Alexander published with permission from the author. Copyright © 1997 Brian Alexander.

Selection from "Shana" by J. Emmett Black, Jr. published with permission from
the author. Copyright © 1997 by J. Emmett Black, Jr.

Selection from "Sheepdog Trials: OK Babe, Try to Match This" by Michael
Cowley reprinted from the April 28, 1997 issue of *The Sydney Morning
Herald*. Reprinted by permission of the author. Copyright © 1997 by
Michael Cowley.

Selection form *The Snow Leopard* by Peter Matthiessen. Copyright © 1978 by
Peter Matthiessen. Used by permission of Viking Penguin, a division of
Penguin Books USA, Inc. and Harvill Publishers.

Selection from "South of the Border with Spot" by Paula McDonald published
with permission from the author. Copyright © 1997 by Paula McDonald.

About the Editor

The first five years of Christine's life were spent in New York City watching retired attack dogs in a neighboring yard snarl and rush the flimsy fence protecting her house. At this point she did not like dogs. However, when the family moved to the country and adopted a puppy from a neighborhood litter, Christine grew out of her fear of dogs as quickly as Duke grew into 90 pounds of fun and affection. Thus began her life-long passion for dogs.

After remaining dog-less just long enough to pick up a college education and a few years of book publishing experience in Boston, Christine moved to California. There she spent six years as a sales representative traveling around the Western United States with her dog, Arthur, who never met a bookseller he didn't like.

These days Christine stays closer to the Northern California home she shares with her husband, two daughters, and two canine kids. Her golden retriever, Willy, is a retired breeder for Canine Companions for Independence, a pet therapy dog, and accompanies Christine on many outings as a volunteer for just about any animal-related cause.

TRAVELERS' TALES GUIDES

LOOK FOR THESE TITLES IN THE SERIES

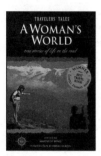

A WOMAN'S WORLD
Edited by Marybeth Bond
ISBN 1-885211-06-6, 475 pages, $17.95

"I loved this book! From the very first story, I had the feeling that I'd been waiting to read these women's tales for years. I also had the sense that I'd met these women before. I hadn't, of course, but as a woman and a traveler I felt an instant connection with them. What a rare pleasure."
—Kimberly Brown, *Travel & Leisure*

A WOMAN'S WORLD and THAILAND, Winners of the Lowell Thomas Award for BEST TRAVEL BOOK
Society of American Travel Writers

THAILAND
Edited by James O'Reilly & Larry Habegger
ISBN 1-885211-05-8, 405 pages, $17.95

"This is the best background reading I've ever seen on Thailand!"
—Carl Parkes, author of *Thailand Handbook,
Southeast Asia Handbook* by Moon Publications

Check with your local bookstore for these titles or
call O'Reilly to order:
800-998-9938 (credit cards only-Weekdays 6 AM –5 PM PST)
707-829-0515, or email: order@oreilly.com

GUTSY WOMEN
TRAVEL TIPS AND WISDOM FOR THE ROAD

By Marybeth Bond
ISBN 1-885211-15-5, 124 pages, $7.95

Packed with instructive and inspiring travel vignettes,
Gutsy Women: Travel Tips and Wisdom for the Road is a
must-have for novice as well as experienced travelers.

GUTSY MAMAS
TRAVEL TIPS AND WISDOM FOR MOTHERS ON THE ROAD

By Marybeth Bond
ISBN 1-885211-20-1, 150 pages, $7.95

A book of tips and wisdom for mothers traveling with
their children. This book is for any mother, grand-
mother, son, or daughter who travels or would like to.

THE ROAD WITHIN

Edited by Sean O'Reilly,
James O'Reilly & Tim O'Reilly
ISBN 1-885211-19-8, 443 pages, $17.95

"A revolutionary new style of travel guidebook."
— *New York Times News Service*

NEPAL

Edited by Rajendra S. Khadka
ISBN 1-885211-14-7, 423 pages, $17.95

"Always refreshingly honest, here is a collection that
explains why Western travelers fall in love with Nepal and
return again and again."
—Barbara Crossette, *New York Times* correspondent and author of
So Close to Heaven: The Vanishing Buddhist Kingdoms of the Himalayas

PARIS

Edited by James O'Reilly,
Larry Habegger & Sean O'Reilly
ISBN 1-885211-10-4, 424 pages, $17.95

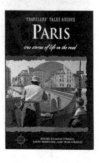

"If Paris is the main dish, here is a rich and fascinating
assortment of hors d'oeuvres. *Bon appetit et bon voyage!*"
—Peter Mayle

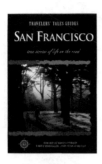

SAN FRANCISCO
Edited by James O'Reilly,
Larry Habegger & Sean O'Reilly
ISBN 1-885211-08-2, 432 pages, $17.95

"As glimpsed here through the eyes of beatniks, hippies,
surfers, 'lavender cowboys' and talented writers from all
walks, San Francisco comes to vivid, complex life."
—*Publishers Weekly*

HONG KONG
Edited by James O'Reilly,
Larry Habegger & Sean O'Reilly
ISBN 1-885211-03-1, 438 pages, $17.95

"*Travelers' Tales Hong Kong* will order and delight the senses, and
heighten the sensibilities, whether you are an armchair traveler
or an old China hand."
—Gladys Montgomery Jones
Profiles Magazine, Continental Airlines

BRAZIL
Edited by Annette Haddad & Scott Doggett
ISBN 1-885211-11-2, 433 pages, $17.95

"Only the lowest wattage dimbulb would visit Brazil
without reading this book."
—Tim Cahill, author of *Jaguars Ripped My Flesh* and
Pecked to Death by Ducks

FOOD
Edited by Richard Sterling
ISBN 1-885211-09-0, 444 pages, $17.95

"Sterling's themes are nothing less than human
universality, passion and necessity, all told in
stories straight from the gut."
—Maxine Hong Kingston, author of
The Woman Warrior and *China Men*

SILVER MEDAL WINNER
BEST
TRAVEL
BOOK
LOWELL THOMAS AWARD

SPAIN

Edited by Lucy McCauley
ISBN 1-885211-07-4, 452 pages, $17.95

"A superb, eclectic collection that reeks wonderfully of gazpacho and paella, and resonates with sounds of heel-clicking and flamenco singing—and makes you feel that you are actually in that amazing state of mind called Iberia."
—Barnaby Conrad, author of *Matador* and *Name Dropping*

FRANCE

Edited by James O'Reilly,
Larry Habegger & Sean O'Reilly
ISBN 1-885211-02-3, 432 pages, $17.95

"All you always wanted to know about the French but were afraid to ask! Explore the country and its people in a unique and personal way even before getting there. Travelers' Tales: your best passport to France and the French!"
—Anne Sengés, *Journal Français d'Amérique*

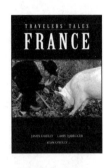

INDIA

Edited by James O'Reilly & Larry Habegger
ISBN 1-885211-01-5, 477 pages, $17.95

"The essays are lyrical, magical and evocative: some of the images make you want to rinse your mouth out to clear the dust."
—Karen Troianello, *Yakima Herald-Republic*

MEXICO

Edited by James O'Reilly & Larry Habegger
ISBN 1-885211-00-7, 426 pages, $17.95

"*Travelers' Tales Mexico* opens a window on the beauties and mysteries of Mexico and the Mexicans. It's entertaining, intriguing, baffling, instructive, insightful, inspiring and hilarious—just like Mexico."
—Tom Brosnahan, coauthor of Lonely Planet's *Mexico: A Travel Survival Kit*